DISCARDED

JUNG and POLITICS

JUNG

The Political and

and POLITICS

Social Ideas of C. G. Jung

Volodymyr Walter Odajnyk

Foreword by Marie-Louise von Franz

New York • NEW YORK UNIVERSITY PRESS • 1976

The first two chapters of this book were published in somewhat different form in *The American Political Science Review* 67, no. 1 (March 1973), under the title "The Political Ideas of C. G. Jung," and are reprinted here by permission.

Passages from *The Collected Works of C. G. Jung,* edited by Gerhard Adler, Michael Fordham, William McGuire, and Herbert Read, translated by R. F. C. Hull, Bollingen Series 20, are reprinted by permission of Princeton University Press.

For Chrystia

Acknowledgments

I want to express my gratitude to Professors Herbert Deane and Julian Franklin, for years my tutors in political theory at Columbia University. They patiently allowed me to develop and pursue my own intellectual interests, and in recent years helped provide the necessary moral and material support. Professor Deane read the first draft of the manuscript and made a number of suggestions that led me to alter the style and manner of presentation. The result, I think, is a more interesting and readable essay. Dr. Marie-Louise von Franz was kind enough to go over the manuscript and bring to my attention a number of questions concerning my interpretation, and was very generous in agreeing to write the Foreword. Finally, I am grateful to Corona Machemer, my editor at Harper & Row, for her insistence on clarity and continuity of expression; her constructive editorial suggestions were invaluable in the preparation of the final version of the manuscript.

I began this study while on a Chamberlain Fellowship from Columbia University during the fall semester of 1971–72. Subsequently a generous two-year postdoctoral fellowship from the Swiss National Science Foundation enabled me to complete my research and writing at the C. G. Jung Institute in Zurich.

V. W. O.

Contents

Foreword

Having known Professor C. G. Jung during the last twenty-eight years of his life, I found it strange to be asked to write a foreword to a book on his political ideas, for his primary interest was in the single human being and not in politics. However, his anthropological studies and his concepts of the archetypes and the collective unconscious did inevitably make him take stands in contemporary political conflicts, and he developed a number of sociological and political ideas. Although Professor Odajnyk has not refrained from honestly giving his own views, he gives in this book a very valuable survey of Jung's attitude toward anthropological and political questions.

Jung always followed contemporary events, but his eye was that of a trained depth psychologist, and he was more interested in looking for what was going on below the surface of everyday political life than in its superficial aspects. Though he was a convinced supporter of the Swiss democracy, I never heard him recommend its constitution as a panacea for all other countries. What he was passionate about were *les droits de l'homme,* the security of man's basic rights and the freedom of the individual, which are guaranteed not only by a "just" state, but far more by the maturity, wisdom, and consciousness of all the members of a community. The individual matters more than the system. Though Jung naturally rejected all forms of dictatorship and tyranny, he did not much believe in forcibly changing a social system before man himself had changed. He never got tired of emphasizing again and again that every change must begin with the individual himself and not with trying to improve other people; the latter he regarded as a display of the power complex. Changes in the individual cannot be brought about by intellectual insight alone; they come from the unconscious, while the "right" or "wrong" attitude of consciousness decides the form of their realization.

Jung took a firm line against any form of intolerance or claims of having the "only" truth. He tried to show that to live unequivocally with one's own inner truth and to tolerate other people's truth were not only reconcilable but essentially identical in the form of an antinomy.

The same antinomy applies to the principle of social relatedness. The relatedness of the individual with his inner Self is coincident with his social relatedness. Nobody can relate to others if he has not first a relationship with his own inner Self. To a great extent all political dissension and conflicts are exteriorizations of inner conflicts that each human being should resolve within himself, thus taking the weight of his neurotic dissociation away from society.

Jung believed that possessed states of psychic inflation and "wrong" emotions in the masses are very infectious. But he was also convinced that a mature attitude toward the powers of the unconscious has a positive effect that spreads to others, a proposition which his own life certainly supported. When he engaged overtly in politics he seldom succeeded, but through his work on the unconscious he has influenced and helped in-numerable people and prevented a lot of disastrous neurotic nonsense from being perpetrated. If ever his more inward-looking attitude toward life should expand—and there are signs that it is doing so—politics would become less of a battlefield of emotions. Already in many areas today the factor of Weltan-schauung—religion and ideology—prevails over pure politics.

From my point of view, Jung stands at the beginning of a great worldwide change in man, a change on which his survival depends, namely a turning inward and toward the irrational creative impulses and manifestations of the unconscious. These are welling up to compensate for the dangerously neurotic one-sidedness of our present-day conscious attitudes. At the core of these unconscious compensatory tendencies lies a new image of man as the Anthropos, a symbol which unites the inner Self of the individual with the Self of mankind as a whole. It appears in the products of the unconscious as a *homo quadratus vel rotundus* (also represented by a mandala), a symbol of an order which brings and holds together the disrupting tendencies of our age. We cannot tell what society will look like when a majority of people will have realized this, but it can only be realized if *les droits de l'homme* are guaranteed, so that the individual can give himself to the task.

Jung thought that we live in a time which is very similar to that of the decay of the Roman Empire and the advent of Christi-anity. Then, out of the collective unconscious and in a despised hidden corner, a new symbol of man emerged, which changed our whole culture in a way that no old Roman politician could have possibly imagined—one need only read Pliny's letter to Trajanus about the new, abstruse sect of Christians to see this. If this change does not come through, or even if it does, Jung foresaw great trouble in the coming years and he was deeply concerned, not about politics in the everyday sense of the word, but about the fate of mankind as a whole. He felt that this was threatened by overpopulation and pollution even more than by wars; but he deeply mistrusted all idealistic-isms, for they are "fronts" for a possessed state of mind. "We must, therefore," he says, "no longer succumb to anything at all, not even to good... Every form of addiction is bad, no matter whether the narcotic be alcohol or morphine or idealism."[1] Only by enduring the conflict of opposites *within himself* and by uniting them in the Self will man be able to survive the present crisis.

MARIE-LOUISE VON FRANZ
November 1974

---

1. C. G. Jung, *Memories, Dreams, Reflections,* ed. Aniela Jaffé (New York: Vintage, 1965), p. 329.

Preface

For over a decade my intellectual interests have been almost fully engaged by political and social philosophy. I assumed that social and political ideas have an important molding influence on the nature of human existence: they supply the basic notions that determine the manner of human life—institutions, inter-actions, aspirations. Without a historical and theoretical grasp of fundamental social and political concepts, I felt that I could not make sense of man's social existence, nor offer considered judgment about the essential principles of that existence—the best form of government, the nature and limitations of liberty, justice, equality, and so on.

In the course of my studies, I was constantly confronted by the fact that every political and social theory, every concept of society, government, and justice rests, in the last analysis, on some conception of human nature. This conception, whether implied or explicitly stated, turned out to be the keystone around which the rest of the theory was constructed, as well as the measure of all other political and social principles and practices: one need only recall the inseparable connection between the respective notions of human nature in Plato, Saint Augustine, Machiavelli, Hobbes, Locke, Rousseau, Bentham, or Mill and their social and political theories, explanations, and ideals. Even in cases where the notion of historical development plays the central role, as in Hegel and Marx for example, a concept of human nature still retains a dominant place in the theory. Faced with these facts, I felt it necessary to undertake an examination of human nature, particularly of human psychology, as it relates to political and social matters.

Of the two great branches of modern psychology, I found the behavioral approach inadequate for explaining the inner motivations of the psyche. Consequently, I turned to Freud and to the psychoanalytic discoveries about the nature of man. But here, although I thought the point of departure valid, I found the method highly subjective, much too one-sided and narrow, and the conclusions inordinately pessimistic. In the aftermath of my disappointment with Freud I turned to Jung.

As this book indicates, I found Jung's conception of human nature much more satisfying than Freud's, and developed a sympathetic feeling for Jung's method, for his essential concepts, and his general world view. Nevertheless, I do not consider myself a "Jungian." As young and as problematical as it is, analytical psychology is a science and not a cult, and I regard myself free to entertain various economic, sociological, and psychological ideas that have nothing to do with Jung. I make an issue of this point only because of the compartmentalization and in-fighting among the various schools of psychology, which result in the pernicious habits of categorizing and labeling, and worse still, in the lazy and dishonest tendency to subsume issues, facts, and theories under a name, and so dispose of them with a word.

Jung never wrote a treatise that systematically defines the implications of his psychological theories for politics. His views on the subject are dispersed throughout his works, although a number of books and essays are closely concerned with politics, either explicitly or by implication and logical extension. Hence, this book represents a compilation of those of Jung's ideas that have political or social implications, gleaned from his voluminous writings on various subjects, a comparison of those ideas with Freud's, and a consideration of just what Jung's ideas imply for the social and political future of humanity.

1

The Origin of Culture and Politics

Jungian psychology accepts and tends to substantiate the biological and anthropological assumption that in his origin man is a herd or social animal. Jung begins his inquiry into the social nature of man with the question of how man became a cultural animal; that is, how he began consciously to develop and pass on religious, aesthetic, and organizational concepts. He approaches the problem of the origin of culture through an examination of the concept of libido, defining it as a general life instinct, or "psychic energy," which is not reducible to the sexual instinct (as in Freud) but includes all human drives—hunger, or the urge to imitate, for instance. Generally speaking, libidinal energy is "apportioned by nature to the various functional systems, from which it cannot be wholly withdrawn," although under certain conditions, "a small part of the total energy can be diverted from its natural flow."[1] This diverted "surplus" energy then becomes available for the development of culture and

1. "On Psychic Energy," volume 8, p. 47. All citations from Jung's writings refer to the first edition of *The Collected Works of C. G. Jung,* Bollingen Series 20 (New York: Pantheon Books; Princeton, N.J.: Princeton University Press, 1964–).

civilization.

Jung maintains that surplus psychic energy must be the product of some sort of tension of opposites, for "there is no energy unless there is a tension of opposites."[2] And he implies that the most generalized form of such tension is that between "matter" and "spirit." Jung does not define these categories, for he asserts that the "ultimate nature of both is transcendental, that is, irrepresentable, since the psyche and its contents are the only reality which is given to us *without a medium.*"[3] It is only on the basis of his examination of the human psyche, its structure and contents, that he postulates these two categories: the existence of matter is attested to primarily by sense perception, while the belief in the existence of spirit is supported by psychic experience. And he maintains that a study of man's history and psyche indicates that a fundamental opposition between matter and spirit exists within human nature. For instance, he thinks that

> man living in the state of nature is in no sense merely "natural" like an animal, but sees, believes, fears, worships things whose meaning is not at all discoverable from the conditions of his natural environment. Their underlying meaning leads us in fact far away from all that is natural, obvious, and easily intelligible, and quite often contrasts most sharply with the natural instincts.[4]

In part, Jung has in mind here various primitive religious beliefs and practices.

A more specific source of tension that accounts for the appearance of surplus psychic energy is the "opposition between the profoundly primitive nature of the newborn infant and his highly differentiated inheritance."[5] The "natural man," for

2. *Two Essays on Analytical Psychology,* volume 7, p. 52. See also volume 8, p. 53.
3. "On the Nature of the Psyche," volume 8, p. 216.
4. "On Psychic Energy," volume 8, p. 52.
5. *Ibid.,* p. 53.

Jung, is characterized by unbridled instinctuality. In time, however, his instinctual nature is thwarted by the inherited "mnemonic deposits accruing from all the experience of his ancestors."[6] These deposits are not inherited *ideas,* but *possibilities* of ideas, potentialities; they are psychic paths traced out by the remote and immediate ancestors of the individual. The individual's mind, therefore, as the "active principle in the inheritance, consists of the sum of the ancestral minds, the 'unseen fathers' whose authority is born anew with the child."[7] The child, of course, is unconscious of this inheritance. It is only aware of the fact that something is interfering with the free expression of its instincts; it projects this internal interference first onto the parents, and later onto society.[8]

The third source of tension that leads to the production of surplus psychic energy is supplied by the parents and society, which play an actual (as well as projected) role in restricting the natural expression of the individual's instincts; in fact, that is how, at least partially, the inherited restrictive dispositions developed in the first place. But why should opposition between the individual's instincts and the demands of the parents and the community still exist if these demands have been passed on through inheritance and therefore internalized by the individual? One explanation is that the individual's instincts, in strength and direction, recapitulate a more primitive stage of

6. *Ibid.*
7. *Ibid.,* p. 54.
8. Given Jung's view of psychological evolution, it really makes no sense for him to assert that the "natural man" is characterized by "unbridled" instinctuality—the "profoundly primitive nature of the newborn infant" seems a more balanced conception. In fact, in Jung's terms, the closer man is to his primitive past, the more his libido is tied to various functional systems and instinctive patterns of behavior from which it cannot be easily withdrawn. A more felicitous expression than "unbridled" instinctuality would be "blind" instinctuality; Jung's essential point could be preserved by stressing the heedless drive and intense power of the primitive instincts. Indeed, it is only with further evolution, when man is able to command and apportion a good part of his libido at will, that "unbridled" instinctuality becomes possible.

human development than that into which he is born. Consequently, his parents and, in adulthood, the society, must inculcate in him modes of behavior that as yet have not been passed on through inheritance. Another possible explanation is that the new modes of behavior have already been passed on through inheritance, but being of recent origin they are not as strong at birth as the earlier instincts and patterns of behavior and come to the fore only with the further maturation of the individual. In this case too, until the later inherited modes of behavior do make their appearance, the parents and the community must oppose those aspects of the individual's behavior that reflects his earlier instincts. And since regression to earlier forms of instinctual behavior is an ever-present possibility, not only for children, but for adults, and even for the community as a whole, the tension between man's primitive instincts and his more developed communal behavior, or ethics, is always present. Therefore, Jung notes, "the conflict between infantile instinctuality and ethics can never be avoided. It is . . . the *sine qua non* of psychic energy."[9]

Thus, the combination of tensions resulting from the opposition between "spirit" and "matter," between the original instincts and the inherited instinct-inhibiting dispositions, and between the individual's instincts and the ethical demands of the society produces that surplus psychic energy which man has at his disposal for the construction of civilization and culture.

There appears to be no simple answer to the question of why man should utilize the excess psychic energy for the development of culture. Jung believes that man's movement in this direction "must be due to something rooted deep in his nature, indeed in the nature of the living organism as such. For living matter is itself a transformer of energy, and in some way as yet unknown

9. "On Psychic Energy," volume 8, p. 56.

life participates in the transformation process."[10] Jung thinks, however, that he is able to account for the psychological mechanism that transforms the surplus psychic energy into cultural manifestations—the *symbol*.

In psychological terms, the symbol is a *libido analogue*, "an idea that can give equivalent expression to the libido and canalize it into a form different from the original one."[11] But the formation of symbols is not a conscious procedure (this is one reason why it is difficult to answer the question about transformation of energy); rather, symbols are "produced out of the unconscious by way of revelation or intuition."[12] Very often they are derived directly from dreams, or are influenced by them. In most cases, the symbols so produced possess a numinous, magical quality: they are highly charged with psychic energy and have an overpowering, compulsive influence. Consequently, when such symbols arise, men frequently objectify them in analogous material or behavioral form: talismans and sacred objects, magic and magical rituals are the first expressions of transformed libidinal energy. The very nature of magical rituals, and of talismans and sacred objects and the actions performed on or around them, clearly indicates their function as transformers of energy. Magic serves as a bridge between the world of symbol and the world of matter: first, it attempts to embody the symbol in the world and so lift the objective realm to a symbolic level—it "spiritualizes" the world; and second, it strives to call forth or revivify the symbolic images so that the energy associated with them will reappear. In time, men discover that the magic ritual can produce the numinosity associated with a symbol and release the desired energy without that symbol's constellation in the psyche of the participant. As this effect is

10. *Ibid.*, p. 41.
11. *Ibid.*, p. 48.
12. *Ibid.*

recognized, the ritual is often deliberately performed to release instinctual and emotional energies and guide them to the desired object or activity; it narrows the psychic field of vision and concentrates the conscious and unconscious forces on the desired ends. By canalizing the psychic energy into an object or an activity, the ritual produces the magical numinosity even without the appearance of the symbol. The numinosity then has a stimulating effect on the imagination, and the mind becomes fascinated, even "possessed." In turn, the fascination usually gives rise to playful, frequently repetitive and rhythmical images, sounds, or actions, which at times lead to the accomplishment of valuable work or the making of important discoveries. The enormous effort normally expended during primitive rituals indicates the difficulty of diverting the libido from its natural and habitual flow into an unaccustomed activity. With further psychic evolution, the act of will, to a certain extent, replaces the magic ritual as the canalizer of psychic energy.

At any rate, Jung argues that it is slowly evolving symbol formation which is responsible for the development of "cultural" ideas and behavior. For instance, after the stage associated with fetish objects, a more sophisticated stage in symbol formation is reached with the totem; and the totem "is closely bound up with the beginnings of tribal life and leads straight to the idea of the palladium, the tutelary tribal deity, and to the idea of an organized human community in general."[13] The implication is that the community begins to reflect and live out its symbols in practice, and that symbols, therefore, are the formative agents of communities and supply both the psychic and the organizational foundations of social life.[14] Jung would

13. *Ibid.*
14. See chapters 3 and 4 of Erik Erikson's *Childhood and Society* (New York: Norton & Company, 1950), for a description of the vital role that symbols and myths play in integrating the life of a society, and of the disintegration of social and individual life when for some reason their validity and authority are undermined.

add that this principle is as true today as it was in primitive societies.

Closely associated with the development of culture and tribal organization is the differentiation of individual from group consciousness. To begin with, the psyche is essentially collective, and there exist no perceptible differences among the members of a community in matters of thought, feeling, and behavior. Moreover, if anything happens which indicates that someone is not of like mind, an immediate disturbance is created: "Nothing arouses so much panic among primitives as something out of the ordinary; it is at once suspected of being dangerous and hostile."[15] One reason for the hostility and panic is the fear of the unknown; when the unknown has to do with human consciousness and behavior, that fear is compounded by the bias for uniformity that the psyche possesses as a result of its long evolution from "a sort of generalized or cosmic consciousness, with complete unconsciousness of the subject," to its first differentiation into group consciousness.[16] When primitive man encounters a phenomenon that discloses a difference or a separation from group consciousness, he must feel this "splitting of the psyche as something unseemly and morbid, just as we do. ... [To his] mind it must ... seem a sin to shatter the divine unity of consciousness that ruled the primal night."[17]

The psyche of the primitive individual, therefore, is "more or less identical with the collective psyche, and accordingly has all the collective virtues and vices without any personal attribution and without inner contradiction."[18] Whatever personal differentiation exists is still in its infancy and for the most part unconscious. Only at a higher stage in the development of group

15. "The Meaning of Psychology for Modern Man," volume 10, p. 137.
16. *Ibid.*, pp. 136–37.
17. *Ibid.*, pp. 139–40.
18. *Two Essays*, volume 7, p. 147.

consciousness does individual consciousness begin to separate itself from the collective psyche.

The gradual emergence of individual consciousness is inevitable in Jung's view, since it is the individual who serves literally as the motor for the production of surplus psychic energy. He is the center around which revolve the various oppositions and tensions—spirit and matter, instinct and inheritance, individual and group—that are conducive to the production of psychic energy. To begin with, these opposing tensions are not strongly charged, and the individual remains unconscious of their conflicting demands; he is able to contain them or to project them onto collective symbols or objects of worship. But with the further evolution of group consciousness and symbol formation, with the corresponding changes in group behavior, and with the resulting new demands made upon the individual's psyche and instincts, the growing opposition between the tension-producing antipodes finally bursts forth into the individual's consciousness. To his surprise and horror, he discovers that it is he himself who embodies the contradiction between the demands of his instincts and the requirements of his psyche and community. "The consequence of this discovery is the conflict of repression. We want to be good, and therefore repress evil; and with that the paradise of the collective psyche comes to an end."[19]

Symbolism and magic play an indispensable role in aiding the development of individual consciousness and personality. "The figure of the medicine-man or chief leads the way: both make themselves conspicuous by the singularity of their ornaments and their mode of life, expressive of their social roles."[20] These outward tokens, as well as the possession of secret signs and

19. *Ibid.*
20. *Ibid.*

rituals, segregate them from the rest of the group. By these means, "the primitive creates around him a shell, which might be called a *persona* (mask)."[21] Initially, it is only while he is wearing the mask or performing his ritual task that the individual is separated from the group. Once the mask is cast off, and the ritual completed, he again returns to the fold of the collective psyche. He does not strictly identify himself with the "persona" that he was during the ritual. He was either "inspired" for a time or simply acted as an agent for the tribe or the spirits. He sees no reason why the possession could not equally occur to someone else or why another properly initiated individual could not act as the agent. It is only at another stage in the evolution of consciousness that the individual begins to identify himself more or less completely with his "persona," and that the group acknowledges him as a distinct individual with unique powers. At that point, his office becomes permanent and often hereditary.

Jung speculates that "the impelling motive in this development is the will to power";[22] but he adds that the building up of individual prestige can only be the result of a collective compromise. Society "needs the magically effective figure" (because of the role that magic plays in releasing and channeling psychic energy, and because such a figure satisfies an archetypal need of the collective unconscious), and "it uses the needful will to power in the individual, and the will to submit in the mass, as a vehicle, and thus brings about the creation of personal prestige."[23] Similarly, because the prestigious, powerful personality is of such paramount importance for the life of the community, it is assiduously guarded against the ever-present possibility that it may regress and dissolve into the collective psyche; for collective thinking, feeling, and effort are less demanding and are experi-

21. *Ibid.* My italics.
22. *Ibid.*
23. *Ibid.*, p. 148.

enced as more natural than are individual functioning and effort.[24] Secrecy and taboos, both carrying magical connotations, are relied upon to forestall such a development, and any violations of the sacred secrecy and taboo restrictions are followed by Draconian punishments. Such measures serve to heighten the individual's self-awareness and ensure the proper performance of his unique tasks.

With the appearance of these manifestations of the continuing evolution of the collective and the individual psyche, there now emerges the possibility of conscious conflict and conscious harmony—in a word, *politics.* All the necessary conditions for the inception of politics are present: the self-consciousness of the group and its conscious separation from other groups (on the basis of different totems and taboos); the individual's awareness of himself as a member of a specific group; the distinction, even if temporary, between the rulers and the ruled; the recognition of legitimate authority; the conscious use of power; and a system of normative demands.

The development of culture and politics through the progressive subjugation of the instinctual nature of man and the gradual differentiation of the collective and individual psyche is a painful process, for it puts the individual at enmity with his original nature, with his instincts and his collective consciousness. This disunity, which in clinical terms is actually a neurosis, is "the hall-mark of civilized man," for he is called upon to "harmonize nature and culture within himself."[25] Even the partial unification of the often disparate elements is not accomplished without periodic "rebellion on the part of the animal nature that thirsts for freedom."[26] Thus, from time to time, Dionysian-like orgies pass like a "wave of frenzy through the

24. *Ibid.*
25. *Ibid.*, p. 18.
26. *Ibid.*

ranks of men too long constrained within the limitations of their culture."[27] However, these periods are then compensated for by an often harsh asceticism or spiritual idealism.[28]

Jung stresses that as a civilized being the European has a history reaching back no more than 2,500 years. Beyond that there is a longer prehistorical period of primitive tribal culture and then "hundreds of thousands of years of neolithic culture, and before that an unimaginably vast stretch of time during which man evolved from the animal."[29] Obviously, then, the layer of culture "must . . . be quite extraordinarily thin in comparison with the powerfully developed layers of the primitive psyche. But it is these layers that form the collective unconscious, together with the vestiges of animality that lose themselves in the nebulous abyss of time."[30] And since "nothing is ever lost," men are, though outwardly civilized, "inwardly... still primitives."[31] Consequently, Jung concludes that "mankind is, in essentials, psychologically still in the state of childhood—a stage that cannot be skipped. The vast majority needs authority, guidance, law. This fact cannot be overlooked."[32] He is skeptical of the Pauline concept of overriding the law to serve a higher purpose; he thinks that is a path for which few are chosen, and they tread it "only from inner necessity, not to say suffering,

27. *Ibid.*
28. Jung has in mind not only the "October Fest" or the Mardi Gras before the onset of Advent and Lent respectively, and the similar socially sanctioned freeing of the instincts in non-Christian cultures, but also the more general historical periods of "licentiousness," such as that of the late Hellenistic period culminating in the Stoic and Christian ideals, that of the Renaissance followed by the Reformation, and that of the Romantic Era followed by Victorianism. He conjectures that presently Western Europe is once again undergoing such a period of "instinctual liberation," which will undoubtedly culminate in a new ascetic ideal. See volume 7, pp. 18–19.
29. "The Role of the Unconscious," volume 10, p. 12.
30. *Ibid.*
31. "On the Psychology of the Trickster-Figure," volume 9, part 1, pp. 268–69.
32. *Two Essays,* volume 7, p. 237.

for it is sharp as the edge of a razor."[33] Not only are the primitive instincts in man still powerful and pressing, so that if not restrained by authority and law they would quickly wreak havoc with the individual and society; but in addition, authority and law, in Jung's view, are *internal* needs of the psyche as a result of its inherited patterns and demands.

33. *Ibid.*

2

Psychic Inflation

Jung's conception of the psyche is highly complex. He maintains that both the conscious and the unconscious contain a personal and a collective element. *Personal consciousness* is composed of immediate sense-consciousness of external and internal stimuli, and of traces of past stimuli that can be brought back to immediate consciousness, all drawn together and unified by a fluctuating, changeable ego-complex.[1] *Collective consciousness* is the prevailing *Weltanschauung* or *Zeitgeist,* composed of the accepted beliefs, biases, attitudes, and principles of a given society or group.[2] The *personal unconscious* contains the following elements: personal experiences that have been forgotten or repressed; traces of external and internal stimuli and combinations of ideas that never reached consciousness, either because they were too weak and indistinct or because they were repressed; all psychic contents that are incompatible with conscious attitudes and appear morally, aesthetically, or intellectually inadmissible; and potential functions of the psyche or the personality that are

1. Volume 8, pp. 323–24.
2. Volume 8, pp. 218–19, 340.

13

not consciously developed.[3] And finally, the *collective uncon-scious* is composed of the inherited instincts and forms of per-ception or apprehension that have never been conscious in the individual and that are not acquired during his lifetime, but are characteristic of an entire group of individuals—family, nation, race, or all mankind.[4]

The collective unconscious is divided into "group" and "uni-versal" layers: to the extent "that human brains are uniformly differentiated, the mental functioning thereby made possible is also collective and universal,"[5] but there are also "differentia-tions corresponding to the race, to the tribe, and to the family, ...at a level that is less deep than that of the 'universal' collective psyche."[6] This means that there is a point where the distinction between the personal and the collective unconscious is very tenuous; it becomes a question of degree and distance. For example, the particular talents and temperament of an indivi-dual are inherited from his most immediate ancestors; therefore they are part of both his personal unconscious (for they are uniquely his) and his collective unconscious (for they are in-herited and do not owe their existence to personal experience). The cultivation and gradual geneological dissemination among many individuals of such once unique characteristics eventually makes up the particular contents of the collective unconscious of the family, the tribe, and the race.

The definition of collective consciousness should make clear that the individual, indeed the society, is usually unconscious of the pervasive influence of the collective unconscious on atti-tudes and behavior; the prevailing Weltanschauung has its roots

3. Volume 8, pp. 133, 151, 311; volume 9, part 1, p. 42.
4. Volume 7, pp. 144–45; volume 8, pp. 137–38, 310.
5. *Two Essays*, volume 7, p. 144.
6. *Ibid.*, p. 270. Here Jung makes a functional distinction in the collective psyche: the *collective mind* represents collective thinking, and *collective soul,* collective feeling.

in the personal and the collective unconscious. Thus, aside from containing *inherited* patterns of apprehension and feeling, the unconscious of a group, nation, or race also contains *cultural* patterns of apprehension and feeling that are a product of its contemporary social state. The separation of these two layers is no easy matter, for one influences the other, and, in time, the contemporary cultural layer passes into the inherited collective unconscious. In fact, the four subdivisions of the psyche cannot be regarded as separate compartments, but must be seen as constantly interacting with each other; the distinctions among them are really matters of degree.

The collectively inherited forms of perception and apprehension Jung calls *archetypes*. The archetypes are psychic correlates of the instincts which Jung describes as the *"instinct's perception of itself...* in exactly the same way as consciousness is an inward perception of the objective life-process."[7] They are "the most ancient and the most universal 'thought-forms' of humanity," although they are as much feelings as thoughts.[8] Other writers have defined them variously as "categories of the imagination," *"representations collectives,"* "elementary" or "primordial thoughts."[9] An archetype is the organizational principle behind physical, biological, and psychological phenomena. As an analogy, what might be called the "carbon archetype" is responsible for the various crystalline forms of carbon molecules; the diamond or the graphite form of the carbon molecule is the external manifestation of the archetype, which is otherwise imperceptible and directly unknowable. In the same way, psy-

---

7. "Instinct and the Unconscious," volume 8, pp. 136–37. Jung states that he has borrowed the idea of the archetype from St. Augustine, and considers the term a paraphrase of the Platonic Forms. See "Archetypes of the Collective Unconscious," volume 9, part 1, p. 4 for Jung's etymology of the term.
8. *Two Essays,* volume 7, p. 65.
9. "The Concept of the Collective Unconscious," volume 9, part 1, pp. 42–43. My italics.

chological archetypes come to consciousness only indirectly, through images and symbols, and in this manner give a definite form to the collectively inherited psychic contents. A good deal of the confusion about what Jung means by "archetype" is due to the fact that he uses the term for both an imperceptible organizational principle, and for the various images in which that principle becomes manifest.

Jung holds that the archetypal symbols and motifs are a product of the combined influence of the originally given structure of the psyche and of the deposits of "constantly repeated experiences of humanity,"[10] that is, of natural and social stimuli that leave behind definite mythological traces in the psyche. All repeated situations, particularly if they call forth an intense emotional response—dangers to the body or the psyche, the magically powerful personality, and so on—give rise to archetypal motifs. Furthermore, once the imprint is made, the archetype acts like an agent that tends "towards the repetition of these same experiences. For when an archetype appears in a dream, in a fantasy, or in life, it always brings with it a certain influence or power by virtue of which it either exercises a numinous or fascinating effect, or impels to action."[11] However, like all natural phenomena, the archetypes carry no ethical connotation but are composed of a mixture of positive and negative, creative and destructive elements. Their constellation, therefore, especially if it remains unconscious, always brings with it a certain amount of ambivalence and danger.

It would be impossible to list all the archetypes that the psyche has at its disposal. Moreover, their formation and constellation is influenced by cultural as well as individual inheritance and conscious dispositions. Nevertheless, there are certain symbols,

10. *Two Essays*, volume 7, p. 68.
11. *Ibid.*, p. 69.

ideas, situations, and figures, which, because of their repeated experience by mankind, have become psychic structures and set into motion an almost universally uniform response. Among archetypal figures are: mother, father, child, maiden, ruler, priest, doctor, teacher, and the four basic feminine and masculine archetypes—the physically or sexually attractive man or woman; the femme fatale and the romantic man; the mother with child and the man active in the world; the wise old man and the wise old woman.[12] Archetypal situations include birth, puberty, courtship, sexual intercourse, marriage, death. Archetypal symbols are legion and provide the material for mythology, religion, dreams, art, and literature. Finally, archetypal ideas are secularized and abstract versions or extensions of symbolic themes; one can trace every influential scientific, philosophical, and sociological idea back to its symbolic source: the notion of libido to mana, for example, or the idea of the First Cause to God, or Communion to Paradise. Jung believes that it is their symbolic archetypal base that accounts for the popularity of such ideas and the fierce emotional commitment many have to them.

Jung summarizes the situation as follows:

Although the child possesses no inborn ideas, it nevertheless has an highly developed brain which functions in a quite definite way. This brain is inherited from its ancestors; it is the deposit of the psychic functioning of the whole human race. The child therefore brings with it an organ ready to function in the same way as it has functioned throughout human history. In the brain the instincts are preformed, and so are the primordial images which have always been the basis of man's thinking—the whole treasure-house of mythological motifs.[13]

12. Jung also asserts that the masculine unconscious is usually personified as a woman (the *anima*) and the feminine unconscious as a man (the *animus*); these two archetypal forms can appear in the guise of any of the female or male archetypal figures.

13. "The Psychological Foundations of Belief in Spirits," volume 8, pp. 310-11. Jung speculates that certain archetypes may also exist in aminals (volume 7, p. 69), and theoretically, therefore, "it should be possible to 'peel' the collective unconscious, layer by layer, until we come to the psychology of the worm, and even of the amoeba" (volume 8, p. 152).

One of the aims of analytical psychology[14] is the integration of the conscious and the unconscious elements of the psyche. Since the unconscious contains both personal and collective aspects, a frequent and apparently unavoidable phenomenon resulting from the conscious assimilation of the contents of the unconscious is the extension of the personality beyond limits appropriate to individuals. The person under analysis suddenly discovers within himself elements of not only his personal unconscious but also the collective unconscious. The assimilation of the personal unconscious may produce a sense of exhilaration, and provide new confidence and strength for the individual. However, since the contents of the collective unconscious also seem to belong to the individual, he may attempt to assimilate these aspects of his psyche and to identify with them. If this happens, he extends his personality beyond his individual limits and "fills a space which he normally cannot fill. He can only fill it by appropriating to himself contents and qualities which properly exist for themselves alone and should therefore remain outside our bounds."[15] As a result of this extension of his personality, the individual experiences a sense of being "superhuman" or "godlike." Jung defines this phenomenon as *psychic inflation.*

Although defined in the context of analytical psychology, the existence of psychic inflation is not confined to therapeutic situations. Nor is it related exclusively to an individual's identification with the contents of the collective unconscious. In the first place, since consciousness is both personal and collective, psychic inflation may also be personal or collective; that is, a group, a nation, or a race may experience psychic inflation. Furthermore, the psychic inflation of an individual may result from his unwarranted identification not only with contents of the col-

14. Jung uses this term to distinguish his theories and his psychotherapeutic method from the "psychoanalysis" of Freud and the "individual psychology" of Adler.
15. *Two Essays,* volume 7, p. 140.

lective unconscious but with any contents—social or metaphysical, for instance—that are beyond the limits of the individual's (or the group's) actual and consciously determined nature and powers. Thus psychic inflation may result from identification with contents of the collective consciousness.[16]

One of Jung's examples of an individual's identification with elements of the collective consciousness is "the humourless way in which many men identify themselves with their business or their titles."[17] The office an individual holds contains collective as well as personal factors. It came into existence through the cooperation of many people, and its dignity or power depends on collective approval. When, therefore, an individual identifies himself completely with his office or title, he makes an extraordinary extension of his personality and usurps qualities that are not in him but outside him. *"L'état c'est moi* is the motto for such people."[18]

This example also illustrates that "transpersonal contents are not inert or dead matter...rather they are living entities which exert an attractive force upon the conscious mind."[19] In other words, not only does the individual seek an identification with the office in order to enlarge his personality, but also the office itself has a power that attracts the individual and entices him to submerge his personal identity in the enlarged collective identity of the office.

One of the dangers of such psychic inflation is the atrophy of the individual personality, so that "underneath all the padding one [finds] a very pitiable little creature."[20] As a result of the individual's identification with the transpersonal qualities and

16. That such identifications also have unconscious, archetypical elements is unavoidable; all behavior is inevitably influenced by the archetypes.
17. *Two Essays,* volume 7, p. 140.
18. *Ibid.*
19. *Ibid.,* p. 142.
20. *Ibid.*

powers of his office a vicious circle develops. On the one hand, such identification is attractive because "it offers easy compensation for personal deficiencies."[21] But, on the other hand, the identification does not allow for the development of the personality, and therefore increases the sense of personal deficiency, which, in turn, strengthens the identification with the compensating transpersonal elements.[22]

Although in Jung's example the individual psyche is extended and "inflated," one could argue that there are instances of identification with social roles that lead to a narrowing of the individual psyche and therefore to psychic "deflation." For instance, the members of the "pariah" or lower classes, or members of socially despised national or racial groups frequently identify personally with their socially defined status and roles; these roles, too, contain transpersonal contents which can influence the conscious and unconscious mind. The result, as in the case of psychic inflation, is the atrophy of the individual personality, which fails to develop beyond the limits imposed by the social role. And, deflationary roles also have their attractive aspects: they offer an easy compensation or justification for personal deficiencies and a psychologically satisfying submergence of the individual in the collective. Religion often provides a form of psychic deflation. When man's better qualities are externalized

21. *Ibid.*
22. Of course the social and political realms could not exist without certain transpersonal or impersonal offices and functions. Nevertheless, not only do these tempt the individual to abandon his responsibility and lose his personality in an inflated identification with his office or duty; in fact, the retention of individual self-awareness, personality, and responsibility is frequently opposed by the bureaucratic aims of objectivity, efficiency, and predictability. Thus, maintaining an antibureaucratic stand is the only way of retaining one's individuality, and decentralization and respect for individual differences are the necessary features of any political system that would safeguard individual responsibility and growth. Under such a system, politics would consist of the tension between the demands of the individual self-realization and social needs. Obviously, given current class, racial, national, and ideological struggles, such a formulation is utopian. But utopian conceptions based on actual human needs have a dynamic and mobilizing force, and their theoretical formulation is not without value.

or projected onto an idol or an extra-mundane Father in Heaven, "the logical result is that the only thing left behind here is a miserable, inferior, worthless, and sinful little heap of humanity."[23]

The proposition that identification with contents outside one's personality may lead to a negative as well as a positive psychic inflation is borne out by Jung's analysis of what happens to an individual's ego when it is assimilated by (identifies with) the unconscious heritage of the collective psyche. Here Jung clearly states that there are two possible reactions to such an assimilation: a feeling of superiority, or a feeling of inferiority. In one individual, the conscious realization of the unconscious contents gives rise to a feeling of superiority and heightened self-confidence, for such realization is not effected without painfully acquired insights and the moral struggle necessary to bring together two disparate spheres that have been anxiously kept apart. In another individual, the newly won insights into the shadow side of his collective unconscious and the recognition of the powerlessness of the ego against the forces of the unconscious produce intense feelings of inferiority and despair. The first person assumes a responsibility for the unconscious that goes much too far, while the second refuses to accept any responsibility whatsoever. One becomes overweening and arrogant; the other becomes overanxious and despondent.[24] Furthermore, Jung thinks that if these two extreme modes of reaction are analyzed more closely, "behind the optimistic self-confidence of the first there lurks an equally deep, or rather far deeper, helplessness, for which the conscious optimism acts as an unsuccessful compensation. And behind the pessimistic resignation of the second there is a defiant will to power, far

23. *Two Essays,* volume 7, pp. 233–34.
24. Jung admits that these are the two extremes of the possible reactions, and that most fall somewhere in between.

surpassing in cocksureness the conscious optimism of the first."[25]

In the realm of politics, the political leader who has inflated his personality through identification with his office, or who feels that he represents the collective will experiences a sense of self-confidence, omnipotence, and megalomania that borders on "godlikeness." According to Jung he is compensating for a deep-seated impotence that expresses itself in this extraordinary way. Moreover, once the identification with the collective contents is established, the development of the individual personality may suffer; this gives rise to an increased sense of personal deficiency, which in turn is compensated for by a greater identification with the collective contents, and so on, in the vicious circle described above. In addition, the sense of personal deficiency often leads to anxiety about the loss of power, which may in turn inspire a paranoid fear of competition from others. All of this may then be compensated for by an intensified will to power, with the end result being political tyranny and, where possible, totalitarianism.

On the other hand, the conscious feeling of impotence and inferiority in men who do not strive for power frequently conceals an unconscious, often pathological, will to power, which may be satisfied by an identification with a powerful, megalomaniacal leader. The identification may be conscious, but it can also occur on the unconscious level, producing passivity, and thwarting any conscious resistance to the powerful leader figure. In addition, the tyrannical control established by such a leader may serve to heighten the sense of inferiority and impotence of the subjects, thereby further strengthening in them the compensatory will to power. If the leader can channel this reaction into an identification with himself and his powers, then the tyr-

25. *Two Essays*, volume 7, p. 136.

anny is fortified; if he is not able to do this, the reaction may burst forth in a rebellion.

Besides the collective contents associated with the feelings of superiority and inferiority, the collective unconscious contains many other contents and pairs of opposites that may be similarly activated and inflated—good and evil, for example. The inflation of either is possible because the collective psyche is made up of a conglomerate of both the virtues and the vices of humanity, and so one man may arrogate to himself the collective virtues, while another takes collective vice as his personal burden. Both are suffering from delusion because the apparently personally possessed virtues and vices are in reality "the moral pair of opposites contained in the collective psyche, which have become perceptible or have been rendered conscious artifically."[26] Prophets and saints, rather than politicians, are prone to this form of psychic inflation, and meditation is the religious method of becoming aware of the contents present in the personal and the collective unconscious.

Another form of psychic inflation occurs when an individual consciously assimilates one of the archetypal figures of the collective unconscious. It has been mentioned earlier that archetypal figures possess a numinous, "charismatic" quality. Jung thinks that this numinous quality of the personified archtypes is partially a result of the primitive's attribution of magical powers to an aspect of his collective psyche, which, because of its development in the psyche over untold ages, is much more powerful than the individual's conscious powers and personality. When an archetypal figure is brought to consciousness, the ego tends to identify with the numinous quality of the archetype, and the individual experiences a sense of superhuman knowledge and power. This feeling is, however, illusory, because, as in other

26. *Ibid.*, p. 147.

forms of psychic inflation, the ego, adulterated with the archetype, has appropriated something that does not belong to it. And while the individual may feel that his ego has mastered the archetypal forces of the unconscious, in fact, his ego has been mastered and possessed by them.

Jung argues, however, that there are cases in which the individual does actually assimilate and master the archetypal figure and become a mana- or a "charismatic" personality. In such cases, "nothing more should happen that is not sanctioned by the ego, and when the ego wants something, nothing should be capable of interfering."[27]

"Mana" is Jung's term for psychic energy, the manifestation and experience of which constitutes the broadest definition of charisma, in modern parlance an important aspect of political leadership.[28] Jung speaks of mana-personalities and mana-movements. Whenever men encounter unusual or unexpected amounts of energy, a mana-situation results; for the presence or display of energy is fascinating to the psyche—it activates the energy archetype, which promotes an awe-inspiring emotional pattern of response. It makes no difference whether the energy is direct or subtle, originates in the external environment or within the psyche, or is a product of unconscious projection. The response is always the same, varying only in degree and modified only by a conscious awareness of what is happening.

The most obvious experience of energy is the experience of physical prowess, speed, or physical activity generally. Here is

27. *Ibid.,* p. 230.
28. The term "charisma" is theological in origin, stemming from reference to the authoritative influence or power bestowed upon certain individuals by the Holy Ghost. The pioneer sociologist Max Weber adopted it and used it as one of the classifications in his three modern forms of legitimate authority—traditional, rational-legal, and charismatic. In its secular use, the term is value free and can be applied to any individual who evokes an emotional and devotional response from a group of followers. It has passed into politics as a sort of modern version of "divine right."

the basis for the general fascination with sports and racing, and with individuals who are dynamic in their speech or movements; here is the reason why, in many cases, leaders are chosen primarily because they display energetic and forceful habits of speech or behavior. This is the most elementary form of election and hero worship, and under primitive conditions there are good functional reasons for it.

Submersion in mass emotions and activity while part of a crowd or a mass "movement" is another popular experience of energy. Here the empirically evident power of the crowd, together with regression to the collective unconscious, with its reservoir of psychic energy, accounts for the compelling nature of involvement. The foundation for such involvement can lie either in external (physical) or internal (psychological) conditions. Mere physical exposure to crowds or to members of a fervent movement produces an experience of mana and tends to cause the psychic regression; or unconscious contents and energy may overpower the psyche when conscious attitudes and traditional ways of doing things are no longer adequate for dealing with the problems of life, which is why mana-movements and mana-personalities arise frequently under new or distressing circumstances, whether environmental or psychological.

The projection of psychic energy is a third general experience of mana. Jung believes that in primitives and children the contents and energy of the unconscious easily overcome consciousness and are readily projected; this is why so many of the events of their life are heavily colored by mana. As ego-consciousness is strengthened, the mana-quality of feelings and of surrounding persons and events becomes more diffuse and rarer. But even a mature ego is not in control of the unconscious, where the archetypes serve as a kind of mold for the accumulation and discharge of psychic energy. Given the appropriate stimuli, they are easily activated and projected. Thus, any time people encounter figures, symbols, or situations that have an archetypal counterpart in the psyche, the appropriate archetype is immediately activated and its psychic energy projected onto the external object. The object or situation then appears to embody a mysterious power or fascination—in a word, mana.

Identification with an archetype, as we have seen, provides another experience of psychic energy. In this instance, an individual or a group extends its ego to include the transpersonal contents of an archetype. Although they may not be aware of it, their ego-consciousness is really possessed by the archetype, and they act out its patterns and experience its extraordinary energy as their own. Such psychically inflated or pseudomana-groups and individuals in turn become suitable objects or "hooks" for archetypal projections from others, so that the original contamination is compounded and intensified.

Finally, rare individuals and groups manage to master and assimilate the psychic energy of certain archetypes and become true mana-personalities and movements. In fact, anyone, Jung asserts, who has conscious access to his unconscious and gains insight into his actions involuntarily exercises an influence on his environment.[29] The deepening and broadening of his consciousness produces the effect of mana with its influence on the unconscious of others. The presence and activity of such an individual, or of such a group of individuals, bear the imprint of mana and are fascinating and compelling for others. Unlike the pseudo-mana-individuals and groups, they are in conscious control of their exceptional psychic energy, able to direct its use, and contain it within human bounds. And obviously, they, too, become targets for archetypal projections so that their power is intensified and their influence extended.

29. *The Undiscovered Self,* volume 10, p. 303.

Jung mentions Napoleon and Lao-tzu as ideal types of true mana-personalities: one the steadfast superman, and the other the sublime sage. In order to distinguish the real from the illusory assimilation of mana, Jung demands empirical evidence that the individual has become as important and powerful in the world as he feels, or that he does in fact exercise unusual personal influence over others. If he feels like a mana-personality, but has no empirical proofs, it is a case of psychic inflation.

There are difficulties that arise, however, when one attempts to empirically distinguish the true mana-personality from the false. Since "the mana-personality is a dominant of the collective unconscious," it is an archetype that takes the form of hero, chief, ruler of men, medicine-man, doctor, saint, or prophet.[30] Consequently, the archetype is activated by and projected onto *anyone* who fills or approximates these positions. And if the person in question is already suffering from psychic inflation because of the adulteration of his ego with an archetypal figure, then the projection supplies him with the empirical evidence needed for him to conclude that he is, in fact, a mana-personality. Furthermore, all projections and beliefs tend to create their own "psychic reality," and their influence may be such as actually to produce or increase the mana-quality in the receiver of the projection. Like the transpersonal contents of an office or a title, projections and beliefs are not inert or merely imaginary forces; they, too, exert a psychic influence upon the conscious and the unconscious mind and alter their structures and functions. Nonetheless, this is still psychic inflation, for the individual so affected identifies with qualities that he does not in fact possess and over which he has no control; on the contrary, the archetypes and the projections possess his ego and function through him. He has become an instrument for the forces of the

30. *Two Essays*, volume 7, p. 226.

collective unconscious.

This complicated psychological interplay helps to explain the mana or the charisma that doctors, teachers, priests, kings, and politicians seem to possess at times, and with which they readily identify, although as individuals they may lack any personally appealing qualities. This is not to deny the possibility that the individual may develop conscious mastery over the unconscious and archetypal forces that at the moment possess him and provide him with the effective mana. But the rule seems to be that possession by an archetype, like personal identification with one's office or title, "turns a man into a flat collective figure, a mask behind which he can no longer develop as a human being, but becomes increasingly stunted."[31] And, therefore, Jung warns that one must beware of the "danger of falling victim to the dominant of the mana-personality. The danger lies not only in oneself becoming a father-mask, but in being overpowered by this mask when worn by another."[32]

The possibility of being overpowered by the archetypal mask when it is worn by another is yet another source of psychic inflation, resulting from identification with an individual who either actually is or merely appears to be a mana-personality. Not all men have the strength to be independent and self-reliant: "The disciple fantasy is perhaps the best they can accomplish," and "the gratifications of the accompanying inflation at least do something to make up for the loss of spiritual freedom."[33] Through his deification of the mana-personality the disciple also waxes in stature: "Does he not possess the great truth...received straight from the Master's hands?"[34] Psychic deflation is an equally possible reaction: the disciple sits modestly "at the Mas-

31. *Ibid.*, p. 232.
32. *Ibid.*
33. *Ibid.*, p. 169.
34. *Ibid.*, pp. 168–69.

ter's feet and guards against having ideas of his own"; he can indulge in infantile fantasies and revert to childish dependence without any loss to himself—"all responsibility is laid at the Master's door."[35] This negative form of psychic inflation, experienced in varying degrees, is widely prevalent. Given the power of the archetypes, men have "an urge to find a tangible hero somewhere, or a superior wise man, a leader and father, some undisputed authority," and so they often "build temples to little tin gods with the greatest promptitude and burn incense upon the altars."[36] Like the chief and the prophet, the disciple and the loyal follower are also primordial images of the collective unconscious.

Finally, let us consider a form of psychic inflation that is especially significant for the understanding of political behavior: collective psychic inflation due to a group identification with contents of the collective unconscious. Here it is the collective or the group-ego that is overpowered by the unconscious contents. It may be that the individual members of the collective already experience a feeling of psychic inflation because of their sense of unity with the group. Both this sense of unity and the psychic inflation that results from it are strengthened by the group's identification with the collective unconscious. Such group unification with the preconscious collective wholeness "possesses a prodigious psychic virulence" and "power of contagion."[37] For "identification with lower and more primitive stages of consciousness is invariably accompanied by a heightened sense of life,"[38] and provides a "new source of power, which may, however, unleash a dangerous enthusiasm."[39] As with the

---

35. *Ibid.*, p. 168.
36. *Ibid.*, p. 231.
37. "On the Nature of the Psyche," volume 8, p. 225.
38. "Concerning Rebirth," volume 9, part 1, p. 126.
39. "The Psychological Foundations of Belief in Spirits," volume 8, p. 315.

individual, so, too, the group's identification with the collective unconscious produces a feeling of universal validity, omnipotence, and godlikeness, which then leads to the forcing of the demands of the unconscious upon others. In this case, moreover, the sense of validity is supported by the unanimity of thought among the members of the group. Any toleration of individual differences is obliterated by the natural propensity of the collective psyche for psychic unity, and the feeling of omnipotence is intensified by the group's actual physical and social force. Clearly, under such conditions, both the individual and the group are deprived of all conscious expression and development; the political and social consequences of such collective psychic inflation are seldom felicitous and hardly democratic.

Since the contents of the collective unconscious are diverse in character, the group, for various reasons, may be drawn to assimilate only certain parts of the unconscious and ignore others: collective virtue or collective vice, collective love and gentleness, or collective hatred and violence. It may also react to its confrontation with the unconscious with a sense either of superiority or inferiority, of optimism or pessimism. But, in any case, the group's collective will to power will be activated and demand expression, at times even in suicidal terms, as the example of Nazi Germany demonstrates.

Archetypes, too, have a collective as well as an individual character: the group united, the group in action, and the group in submission to a leader, for example, are complements of the more individual archetypes of the family, the medicine-man, and the ruler. Upon assimilating these archetypal contents into its collective consciousness, the group, like the individual, feels that it has come to possess the charismatic, manalike quality of the archetypes. The sense of omnipotence and godlikeness already present because of the group's initial submergence into the preconscious collective wholeness is strengthened by the contact with archetypal elements. Further, if empirical efficacy and actual influence are the criteria of charisma, then, given the power of a large unified group, the criteria often seem to be established. In addition, others who are not members of the group may project their unconscious forces upon the group, thereby increasing its sense of mana-possession and perhaps even effectuating its charismatic powers. The effectiveness of mana-personalities and groups must be judged finally in historical terms; nevertheless, the powers awakened by the group's identification with the contents of the unconscious and by the projections of others may be of such dimensions that it is difficult to determine by external evidence alone whether it is a true or a pseudocharismatic group. The conclusive test is psychological. If the group's sense of charisma and power is due to external projections and to its possession by the collective archetypes, then it is a pseudocharismatic group. It is a victim of psychic inflation, for it identifies with contents that it neither possesses nor controls. It is ruled by the forces of the unconscious and merely acts out its collective images and needs. Since, however, the conscious mastery of the archetypal elements of the unconscious is possible for individuals, it should also be possible for groups. In such cases, real mana-personalities and groups emerge: psychic inflation comes to an end, and the individuals or the groups actually do embody and control the qualities with which they identify.

But cases such as these are extremely unusual, and therefore Jung concludes that they are exceptions that might be said to prove a natural psychic law: psychic inflation results from an individual's or a group's identification with the forces of the collective unconscious and the "naive concretization of primordial images."[40] Almost never, in Jung's view, is it possible to alter the law and so to escape the power of the collective unconscious. "One can only alter one's attitude and thus save oneself from naively falling into an archetype and being forced to act a part at the expense of one's humanity."[41] The individual must confess his "weakness in face of the powers of the unconscious," for "when the ego makes no claim to power there is no possession."[42] In order to achieve this alteration of attitude, however, it is first of all necessary to become aware of the forces of the unconscious. Jung believes that, unfortunately, the social and intellectual developments of the past four centuries in Europe have tended to repress Western man's awareness of both the personal and the collective unconscious. The repression has energized the unconscious and, in view of the neglect of the personal unconscious, the collective unconscious is brought to the fore. The discharge of its pent-up energy takes the form of mass psychoses, which, because of the postenlightenment secular orientation of society, appear as political movements.

40. *Two Essays*, volume 7, p. 231.
41. *Ibid.*, p. 232.
42. *Ibid.*, pp. 232, 228.

3

Mass Psyche and Mass Man

Jung believes that the historical developments that have shaped the contemporary life and consciousness of Western man during the last four centuries have produced both a mass psyche and a mass man. Before the Reformation, in Jung's view, Western man's psyche enjoyed a certain wholeness and equilibrium; for despite its faults, the Medieval religion, with its friendly and fiendish symbols, provided a salutory outlet for the unconscious and irrational forces of the psyche. And prior to the Industrial Revolution, each man's life was bound in a close and personal relationship with nature and with other men.

The Reformation, the Enlightenment, and the Industrial Revolution together have caused a progressively widening cleavage between Western man's conscious and unconscious existence. The universal "neurosis" of mankind, which stems from his having to accommodate in every society the conflicting demands of nature and culture, was further aggravated as the Industrial Revolution removed Western man farther and farther from contact with nature. The result was to divorce him from communal life, isolate him, and destroy his individuality. From the psychological side, neglect and repression of the instincts and of the unconscious energized the collective irrational forces and gave rise to a mass psyche and to collective psychic inflation. From the sociological side, isolation and atomization of individuals produced mass man and the collectivist society and state.

The main impact of the Reformation was to shatter the authority of the Roman Church. Although one result was an increase in the earthly importance of the individual, which later found expression in the modern political ideals of equality, democracy, and social welfare,[1] at the same time there was a gradual accretion of power to the state as it took over functions previously performed by the Church. The Reformation brought religious, intellectual, political, and social confusion and strife. The European, accustomed to patriarchal and hierarchal order, turned to the state to provide it. He projected the displaced "paternal imago" upon the state, and in time came to regard it —as he once had the Church—as "the authority responsible for all thinking and willing," and as "the universal provider," although now in a more material sense.[2] From its side, the state assumed "the age-old totalitarian claims of theocracy, which are inevitably accompanied by the suppression of free opinion,"[3] and eventually made an attempt to "nationalize" religion, and later, at times, to suppress it altogether.

During the Enlightenment, attempts were made to salvage and extend the more humane intellectual and social principles of the Reformation, and the personal and immediate authority of Reason was substituted for traditional and external authority. In the process, however, the powers of the state were further strengthened. The mystical, sacramental administration of the Church was replaced by the rational, secular administration of

1. "The Meaning of Psychology for Modern Man," volume 10, p. 153.
2. "Psychotherapy Today," volume 16, p. 104.
3. "Epilogue to *Essays on Contemporary Events,*" volume 10, p. 231.

the state, and feudal privilege fell to an impersonal, centralized rule. Moreover, the Enlightenment's philosophical stress on individualism, equality, and democracy, with their tendencies toward egoism, selfishness, and anarchy, produced a "compensatory reversion to the collective man"—the rise of socialism and communism. The anarchy of individualism and the resulting formlessness of the collective necessitated the emergence eventually of the absolute monarch or dictator who would either pander to, manipulate, or tyrannize the masses.[4]

From the psychological point of view, the period's overemphasis on rationalism and its rejection of "superstition" brought about the repression of the irrational, unconscious contents of the psyche. Defining the psyche as a tabula rasa, Enlightenment philosophers refused to recognize that the old religions with their sublime and ridiculous, their benevolent and malevolent symbols, did not come from nowhere but were born of the soul that still dwells within us: "All those things, their primal forms, live on in us and may at any time burst in upon us with annihilating force, in the guise of mass-suggestion against which the individual is defenseless."[5] In other words, the Enlightenment may have dethroned the gods and destroyed the spirits of nature, but it did not erase "the psychic factors that correspond to them, such as suggestibility, lack of criticism, fearfulness, propensity to superstition and prejudice."[6] Moreover, Jung notes that in Europe Christianity was originally imposed upon essentially primitive people. The effect was to split the barbarian's psyche in two, and by repressing the lower half enable him "to domesti-

4. All these factors were already apparent in Rousseau's *Social Contract* and visible in the French Revolution and its aftermath. The mass democracies and totalitarian regimes of the twentieth century are merely extensions and "technological" improvements on the earlier developments. See J. Talmon, *The Origins of Totalitarian Democracy* (New York: Praeger, 1961).

5. *Two Essays,* volume 7, pp. 202–3.

6. "After the Catastrophe," volume 10, p. 211.

cate the brighter half and fit it for civilization. But the lower, darker half still awaits redemption and a second spell of domestication."[7] By undermining the authority of Christianity and by ignoring the unconscious and denying its irrational aspects a cultural mode of expression, the Enlightenment intensified the general neurotization of modern man; for "when any natural function...is denied conscious and intentional expression, a general disturbance results."[8] For the Western man such a situation was and is especially dangerous because, Jung believes, the repressed elements in him are of a highly primitive, violent, and cruel nature. The repressed contents become psychically charged and volatile as a consequence of their repression and take their "revenge" by returning in the form of various cults, crazes, crudities, and, in the modern era, *isms*. "Our fearsome gods," writes Jung, "have only changed their names: they now rhyme with—*ism*."[9] And he contends that the diverse modern isms "are only a sophisticated substitute for the lost link with psychic reality," that is, with the forces of the unconscious.[10] They give expression to and mobilize exactly those irrational drives that have been repressed and distorted by the one-sided stress on rationalism and intellectualism. Furthermore, they lead to an identification of individual consciousness with the collective consciousness embodied in the ism "of choice"; this in turn strengthens the group identification with the forces of the collective unconscious. Such an amalgamation "infallibly produces a mass psyche with its irresistible urge to catastrophe."[11]

Although the Enlightenment enhanced individual autonomy and dignity on the basis of the supposed universal capability of

7. "The Role of the Unconscious," volume 10, p. 13.
8. *The Undiscovered Self,* volume 10, p. 280.
9. *Two Essays,* volume 7, p. 203.
10. "On the Nature of the Psyche," volume 8, p. 222.
11. *Ibid.,* p. 221.

every man to reason, ironically the very emphasis on Reason eventually served to undermine the individual. For the Enlightenment's espousal of Reason led to the current Zeitgeist of "scientific rationalism," which aids mass-mindedness by reducing the individual, and indeed all individual events, to abstract statistical units. The individual is perceived to be an anonymous interchangeable member of the collective, a mere contributing unit of a mass organization. And, "looked at rationally and from outside, that is exactly what he is, and from this point of view it seems positively absurd to go on talking about the value or meaning of the individual."[12] In fact, it is difficult to imagine how individual life ever came to be endowed with so much dignity. Instead of the concrete individual, there are only "the names of organizations and, at the highest point, the abstract idea of the State as the principle of political reality."[13] And since the bias of rationalism is for the objective, modern man looks at reality empirically and, seeing the immense power in fact of large organizations and the state, "has nothing with which to combat the evidence of his senses and his reason."[14]

Jung argues that it is an error to follow the rationalistic principles of the Enlightenment to their logical conclusion and attempt to subject all personal and social phenomena to a rational

12. *The Undiscovered Self,* volume 10, p. 253.
13. *Ibid.,* p. 252.
14. *Ibid.,* p. 254. Jung maintains elsewhere that any Zeitgeist tends to stunt individual consciousness and development. The spirit of any age influences the majority of men and gives rise to the characteristic "collective consciousness" of the period. This has nothing to do with rational categories, even though rationalism may be one of the notions of a particular Zeitgeist. A Zeitgeist "is more a bias, an emotional tendency that works upon weaker minds, through the unconscious, with an overwhelming force of suggestion that carries them along with it. To think otherwise than as our contemporaries think is somehow illegitimate and disturbing; it is even indecent, morbid, or blasphemous and therefore socially dangerous for the individual" ("Basic Postulates of Analytical Psychology," volume 8, p. 340). And if, at times, issues develop that raise doubts about the collective wisdom of the time, the collective consciousness usually "wins hands down with its 'reasonable' generalities that cause the average intelligence no difficulty whatever" ("On the Nature of the Psyche," volume 8, p. 218).

will. He thinks that it has never been shown that life and the world are rational; on the contrary, there are "good grounds for supposing that they are irrational, or rather that in the last resort they are grounded beyond human reason. ... Hence reason and the will that is grounded in reason are valid only up to a point."[15] Beyond that point, reason excludes the irrational possibilities of life, thus engendering distortions, and then is surprised and overpowered by the compensations that such distortions beget. Thus, theoretically, reason should be able to put an end to the continued development and stockpiling of nuclear weapons, as well as to the irrational and inefficient manner of solving international problems through war. But if the history of this century has demonstrated anything, it is that reason alone is not enough.

The Industrial Revolution, following upon the heels of the Enlightenment and putting its rational and scientific theories into practice, served to separate Western man even further from his unconscious and instinctual nature. It turned out that the more power man gained over nature, the more his knowledge and skill went to his head, and the deeper became his contempt for the merely natural and accidental, for all irrational data—including the unconscious part of the psyche.[16] It seems that nothing interferes with the connection between the conscious and the unconscious parts of the psyche more than external success and power. Jung often refers to the Gilgamesh epic as an illustration of the psychology of the power complex: he sees the epic as an allegorical description of the relationship between the conscious (Gilgamesh) and the unconscious (Enkidu) aspects of the psyche in a situation where the conscious seeks to dominate all, including the unconscious.[17] In many respects, modern

15. *Two Essays,* volume 7, p. 48.
16. *The Undiscovered Self,* volume 10, p. 291.
17. *Symbols of Transformation,* volume 5, p. 298.

man is repeating the Gilgamesh epic, and, as with our knowledge of that epic, the end is yet unclear.[18]

Jung also notes that man's psychic evolution has not kept pace with intellectual developments, and that the rapid growth of consciousness through science and technology has left unconscious and moral forces far behind. At the same time, the many-sided attacks on the unconscious have forced it into a "defensive position which expresses itself in a universal will to destruction";[19] that is, the unconscious seeks in turn to destroy a world that seems bent on the destruction of the unconscious. In this respect, Jung views the development of nuclear weapons as partially the work of the unconscious; for the unconscious, through hunches and intuitions, collaborates in inventions and discoveries, and "if it puts a weapon in your hand, it is aiming at some kind of violence."[20]

Lastly, the Industrial Revolution concretized the separation between man's conscious and instinctual natures and contributed to the emergence of the mass psyche by uprooting large portions of the population and herding them together into massive urban centers, where, torn from the soil and engaged in one-dimensional employment, they lost, in Jung's opinion, every healthy instinct, including that of self-preservation.[21]

Thus, the final product of the combined forces of the Reformation, the Enlightenment, and the Industrial Revolution is

18. The Gilgamesh epic is a work of some 3,000 lines, written about 2000 B.C., and discovered on fragments of stone tablets among the ruins of Nineveh. It tells of the adventures of the warlike and imperious Gilgamesh, in Babylonian legend, King of Erech, and his primitive counterpart, rival, and friend, Enkidu. When Enkidu suddenly dies, Gilgamesh becomes obsessed with the fear of death. He embarks on a search for a plant which will give eternal life, but finds it only to leave it unguarded so that it is stolen by a serpent. He then turns to the ghost of Enkidu for comfort, but his friend gives him a gloomy view of the future that awaits the dead.

19. "A Study in the Process of Individuation," volume 9, part 1, p. 349.

20. The Undiscovered Self, volume 10, p. 298.

21. "The Fight with the Shadow," volume 10, p. 222, and "After the Catastrophe," volume 10, p. 200.

the *mass man*—a man isolated socially from other men, separated from his unconscious and his instincts, and therefore vulnerable to psychic epidemics, of which mass political movements are the most characteristic and virulent manifestion. In fact, Jung states that he could easily "construct a political theory of neurosis, in so far as the man of today is chiefly excited by political passions."[22] The developments responsible for the peculiar psychic and social disturbances of modern man are also responsible for the fact that he seeks an outlet and a solution for these disturbances in politics. Because of the rationalistic and empirical Weltanschauung of the Enlightenment, religion lost its role as a meaningful force capable of dealing with psychic and social problems. Moreover, the Enlightenment view of the psyche as a tabula rasa logically demands that mankind seek the source of all good and evil in the objective environment. Therefore, even when problems are clearly psychological in origin, the cry still goes up for political and environmental change to solve them. In addition, because of Western man's social isolation and psychic alienation, there exists a need for some sort of unifying element to collect the separated individuals and give expression to their instinctive and unconscious drives. The political movement satisfies this need as well.

In a way, the modern orientation toward the political to solve psychological and social problems seems valid, for it was the particular development of Western society and the state that led to Western man's present social and psychological difficulties. Even in Jung's analysis, it is perceived that political and environmental changes do have a very real effect upon man's psychological condition. Jung's point, however, is that such alterations, if they do not take into account the unconscious and irrational aspects of the psyche, are, at best, meaningless, and, at worst,

22. *Two Essays*, volume 7, p. 19.

dangerous. Thus, although they may alleviate certain pressing problems, political movements do not really solve them, and in fact, have a number of pernicious effects. For instance, by uniting individuals into groups, political movements constellate the forces of the collective unconscious and produce the harmful effects associated with psychic inflation. And because modern man's unconscious has been repressed, its primitive, irrational, and violent contents are psychically strongly charged, so that when they are finally released through a political movement they tend to wreak havoc with both the individual personality and the society.

Moreover, the very *size* of a movement has a detrimental impact upon individual and collective consciousness and behavior: groups exert a seductive influence on their members and entice them to mutual imitation and dependence, and the larger the group, the greater the influence. For "where the many are, there is security; what the many believe must of course be true; what the many want must be worth striving for, and necessary, and therefore good."[23] Unfortunately, however, the morality of a group or of a society is, in Jung's view, in inverse ratio to its size; for the greater the aggregation of individuals, the more are individual moral factors blotted out, and the more does every single member feel absolved of all responsibility for the actions of the group. Consequently, "any large company composed of wholly admirable persons has the morality and intelligence of an unwieldly, stupid, and violent animal. The bigger the organization, the more unavoidable is its immorality and blind stupidity *(Senatus bestia, senatores boni viri)*."[24]

Jung here concurs with Gustave Le Bon's contention that when in a crowd the individual sinks to a primitive moral and

23. *The Undiscovered Self,* volume 10, p. 277.
24. *Two Essays,* volume 7, p. 150.

intellectual level. In Jung's terms, this is the level of the primordial collective unconscious, which is activated by the formation
of a mass; for "everything that exceeds a certain human size
evokes equally inhuman powers in man's unconscious."[25] Many
factors seem to be at work here: the group's influence on the
individual's conscious and unconscious psyche through suggestion; the instinctive human propensity for imitation; the less
demanding intellectual and moral nature of collective thinking
and acting; the "gentle and painless slipping back into the kingdom of childhood, into the paradise of parental care...and
irresponsibility";[26] the tendency of the psyche to revert to its
origins in group consciousness; and the mobilization of the
numinous archetypal contents of the collective unconscious.
Some of these regressive effects of crowd psychology can be
partially countered through ceremonies and rituals: "By engag-
ing the individual's interest and attention, the ritual makes it
possible for him to have a comparatively individual experience
even within the group and so to remain more or less conscious."[27]
But where ritual, or some other focus for the individual's consciousness—for example, the responsibility of holding an office
in an organization—is absent, his own psyche is inevitably
drowned in collective experience and behavior. Perhaps a distinction ought to be made here between the spontaneous crowd
and the large permanent organization such as the Church, the
Army, or the Political Party, but in fact their effect upon the
individual and his psychological response to either are often
the same.[28]

Severed from the Church, from the communal and economic

25. "The Fight with the Shadow," volume 10, p. 226.
26. *The Undiscovered Self,* volume 10, p. 277.
27. "The Psychology of Rebirth," volume 9, part 1, p. 127.
28. See Sigmund Freud, *Group Psychology and the Analysis of the Ego,* in volume 18
of *The Standard Edition of the Complete Psychological Works of Sigmund Freud*
(London: The Hogarth Press, 1955).

security of the guilds, and placed in an urban environment composed of masses of atomized isolated individuals, modern man is especially prone to mass psychic epidemics. Not even his physical presence in a group is required for such epidemics to break out.[29] Modern man, therefore, is a mass man; and masses, being anonymous and irresponsible, and having their archetypal contents activated, necessarily seek, and find, a leader. The leader then gives them a sense of direction, and says, like Hitler, "I take over the responsibility!"[30]

Jung's appraisal of the major developments of Western history during the past four and a half centuries, whose outline serves as an explanation of the present psychological and political condition of Western man, is obviously not a positive one. Neither is it original.[31] The critical, pessimistic view of Western civilization became common among European aristocrats and liberal democrats of Jung's generation, particularly because of the disillusionments associated with the First World War and the Bolshevik Revolution. Fascism and the Second World War merely strengthened that reaction; much of Jung's argument is presented in a more detailed and comprehensive fashion by Ortega y Gasset in *Revolt of the Masses* (1930).

What is original with Jung, however, is the examination and critique of the cultural, socioeconomic, and political develop-

29. Jung has in mind here the panic that followed the 1938 radio broadcast of H. G. Wells's *War of the Worlds* in New York and later in Quito, Ecuador. The Nazi case is another example, although Hitler understood the effects of mass meetings, agitation, and propaganda and utilized them to arouse as well as to direct the collective response of the Germans.

30. "After the Catastrophe," volume 10, p. 201.

31. There are clear intimations of the critique in the work of Jung's compatriot, Jacob Burckhardt (1818–1897). Jung was a student at the University of Basel, where Burckhardt was the authority of the day. Similar attitudes are also found in Gustave Le Bon's *The Crowd* (1895).

ments of the times from the standpoint of what he considers to be the needs of the psyche. It is not that he hankers after the Medieval Church, but that he thinks that that Church provided an orderly outlet for the irrational and unconscious life of the psyche. Similarly, it is from this standpoint that Jung is critical of the rationalistic attitudes of the Enlightenment. And his argument with science and industrialization is that they tend to stress conscious mastery and power, and cut man off from contact with nature, with his instincts, and his unconscious. Add to all this the effects of urbanization and overpopulation, and the result, in Jung's view, is a collection of isolated, alienated, powerless, neurotic individuals whose only collective form is the mass. Mass neurosis breeds mass psychosis, and hence the "mass psychic epidemics," which, for historical and sociological reasons, take the form in modern Western society of mass political movements. Jung's purpose is to add the psychological dimension to an understanding of contemporary politics; he is not particularly concerned with the economic and ideological forces that have also contributed to the nature of political movements in the twentieth century.

Because his emphasis is on the psychological as a counterweight to the modern emphasis on the socioeconomic, Jung is not always interested in exploring the interaction between the two, nor in earlier historical examples of mass psychic epidemics. For such epidemics are not a unique product of the present century, and they need not always take a political form. The Crusades and the numerous millenarian movements of the Middle Ages are also instances of mass psychic inflation. The presence of a religion that allows for the expression of irrational and unconscious forces is not alone sufficient to prevent mass psychoses; the movements simply take a religious form.

There does seem to be evidence, however, that the medieval

millenarian movements were responses to socioeconomic conditions very similar to those brought about by the Industrial Revolution.[32] The increase in population and the rise of commerce and the textile industry during the eleventh through the thirteenth centuries brought with them a by now familiar chain of events: increased social mobility, the breakup of communal ties, the disruption of traditional norms and authority, extremes of wealth and poverty, a surplus of labor, masses of unemployed with no recognized place in society, the rise of a déclassé low-grade intelligentsia, chronic economic insecurity and social frustration, and the absence of any regular institutionalized methods of voicing grievances and pressing claims. Such a situation, then as now, gave rise to a mass of isolated, unstable, alienated, anxious, powerless, and despondent individuals. Any disturbing, frightening, or exciting event—a war, a revolt, a summons to a crusade, an economic depression—acts on these rootless and desperate men in a particular way: in Jung's terms, it constellates the collective unconscious. The crisis calls forth a mass response, a "psychic epidemic," in the form of a messianic movement led by an authoritarian, charismatic leader who makes glowing promises of economic security, equality, and happiness, either in this world or in the world to come. Given historical variability, the intensity and the form of these developments and responses differ greatly. But the general pattern can be readily discerned in a great number of mass movements, from early Christianity to the contemporary nationalist movements in the Third World.

Of course, the fact that psychic epidemics are not unique to twentieth-century Europe does not invalidate Jung's psychological analysis. It merely illustrates that socioeconomic conditions

32. See Norman Cohn, *The Pursuit of the Millenium: Revolutionary Millenarians and Mystical Anarchists of the Middle Ages* (London: Temple Smith, 1970). See especially chapter three and the conclusion.

influence psychological states and responses, just as psychological forces, once in play, have an important effect upon socioeconomic conditions. The point to keep in mind is their close and intimate interaction. With this caveat, we now turn to Jung's further elaboration of the effects of contemporary politics on the psyche.

4

The Individual and the State

Having described Jung's conception of the historical evolution of the mass man, we can now proceed to his more detailed examination of the relationship between the individual and the modern state. Most of his views on this topic are found in *The Undiscovered Self*. The book was written almost incidentally in the spring of 1956, when Jung was already in his eighties, and there was talk of a "thaw" in the political relations between East and West. He openly acknowledged its subjective nature: it is an expression of his personal opinions on issues raised by contemporary world conditions. The book does, however, contain attitudes and ideas that are consistent with his other writings on the individual and society. And although in the course of his exposition he does not always provide the psychological basis for his opinions, these opinions are nevertheless grounded in his understanding of the human psyche. I only raise these matters because on the surface the book may appear to be just another Western liberal's attack on socialism, mass democracy, and political fanaticism, and yet another call for a return to self-reliance, individualism, and spiritual awareness. The fact is that

Jung's understanding of the psyche leads inevitably to the espousal of certain classical liberal ideals, especially the emphasis on the dignity of the individual, the development of his unique capabilities, and the struggle against arbitrary political or social compulsion. It is no accident that the man who spent a good part of his life grappling with the powers of the collective unconscious should take a stand against the submergence of the individual in any collective, be it psychological or social. It was in that struggle that he learned to respect the resources and the creativity of the individual and came to recognize the necessity of developing his awareness and potentialities. He saw that happiness, contentment, equanimity of mind, and meaningfulness of life were achievements of individuals, and not of the collective, and consequently was not much interested in "integrating" the individual into society, certainly never into the mass society he saw developing both East and West of Switzerland.

As we saw in the last chapter, after the Reformation the state assumed the administrative and paternalistic functions of the Church; thanks to the influence of the Enlightenment, it strengthened its administrative machinery through a centralized, rational bureaucracy, and became the sole determinant of morality and law; lastly, as a result of the cultural and social effects of the Industrial Revolution, a mass man was created whose social needs led to the development of a welfare or a socialist state, and whose psychological needs gave rise to arbitrary and absolute dictatorships.

Jung argues in *The Undiscovered Self* that the absolute state to which the individual looks for salvation from his growing social and psychological impoverishment in fact proceeds to destroy every remnant of individuality. The destruction begins innocently enough with intellectual and material paternalism: "All the thinking and looking after are done from the top; to all questions there is an answer, and for all needs the necessary provision is made."[1] The individual is slowly deprived of initiative and self-reliance. He no longer makes any decisions about how he should live his life, "and instead is ruled, fed, clothed, and educated as a social unit, and amused in accordance with the standards that give pleasure and satisfaction to the masses."[2] As a result, he soon loses the capacity for introspection and feels totally dependent on his environment. "He thinks the meaning of existence would be discovered if food and clothing were delivered to him gratis on his own doorstep, or if everybody possessed an automobile."[3] Instead of concern for individual mental and moral development, all attention is centered on the promotion of public welfare and the raising of the living standard. Because individual development becomes secondary to the policy of the state, the decisions of the state take the place of the moral responsibility of the individual: "His code of ethics is replaced by a knowledge of what is permitted or forbidden or ordered."[4] And in keeping with the collective nature of the state, all responsibility is collectivized, that is, relinquished by the individual and delegated to a corporate body. This gradual erosion of man's capacity for self-reliance and individual responsibility begins in school, continues in the university, and pervades all areas of social life. In time, the individual becomes a mere *function* of the society, while the society, enveloped by the state, is turned into a quasi-animate personality and usurps the life-carrying role of the individual. Under these circumstances, how, Jung asks, can one expect a soldier, for example, "to subject an order received from a superior to ethical scrutiny? He has not yet made the discovery that he might be capable of spontaneous

1. *The Undiscovered Self,* volume 10, p. 277.
2. *Ibid.,* p. 252.
3. "On the Psychology of the Trickster–Figure," volume 9, part 1, p. 267.
4. *Ibid.*

ethical impulses, and of performing them—even when no one is looking."[5] When the ethical decisions of the individual no longer guide activity, only the blind movement of the masses remains; to move the masses, lies and half-truths are needed, and these then become the operative principles of political action.

Jung admits that given the economic and social repercussions of the Industrial Revolution, the welfare state is probably necessary and is beneficial in many respects. However, as can be surmised from the above comments, he regards it as a mixed blessing. One of the most detrimental aspects of social welfare "from the cradle to the grave" is that by depriving man of the necessity to struggle for survival, it causes the atrophy of his most vital instinct, the instinct for self-preservation. And "once a man is cut off from the nourishing roots of instinct," especially from the instinct for self-preservation, he becomes a "sick animal, demoralized and degenerate . . . and the shuttlecock of every wind that blows."[6] He loses his self-respect, his joy and interest in life, his will to live, and only a catastrophe of some kind can bring him back to life. Moreover, in the infantile dream stated induced by his total dependence upon the government, he never bothers to ask who is paying for his paradise. "The balancing of accounts is left to a higher political or social authority, which welcomes the task, for its power is thereby increased," and unfortunately the more power it has, the weaker and more helpless the individual becomes.[7] Often he does not realize that dependence on the state really means that everybody is relying on everybody else instead of upon himself. In his preoccupation with his own demands, he fails to see that the state is made up of the very individuals who make the demands. The inevitable

5. *Ibid.*
6. "After the Catastrophe," volume 10, p. 201.
7. *The Undiscovered Self,* volume 10, p. 277.

result of such total dependence is communism, where, in Jung's opinion, every individual enslaves every other individual in the community, and the community comes to be represented by a dictator, a slave driver. "All primitive tribes," Jung writes, "characterized by a communistic order of society also have a chieftain over them with unlimited powers."[8] He concludes that the modern communist state is nothing but an absolute monarchy in which there are no subjects but only serfs.

Thus the trend of contemporary social and psychological conditions is toward political tyranny. Once on the scene, the tyrannical state, because of its immorality, ruthlessness, and disregard of the individual, is soon seen to have tactical and organizational advantages over the democratic state. In order to protect itself, the democratic state may be forced to adopt the same attitudes and behavior as its opponent; this development is made more probable by the importance that is "attached to large numbers and to statistical values, as is everywhere the case in our Western world."[9] The result is that, even in the democratic state, the power of the masses is exalted and respected, while at the same time, "the insignificance of the individual is rubbed into him so thoroughly that he loses all hope of making himself heard."[10]

Thus, contrary to the popular Western notion that communist dictatorships result from the imposition of ideological and political rule "from the top," Jung argues that they are really a product of the social and psychological condition of the masses. In a way, his analysis is curiously Marxist: collective consciousness and political structures reflect cultural and socioeconomic evolution—communism is the product of Enlightenment assumptions and the Industrial Revolution. Jung, however, does

8. "The Psychology of Rebirth," volume 9, part 1, p. 127.
9. *The Undiscovered Self,* volume 10, pp. 277–78.
10. *Ibid.,* p. 278.

not admit that communism is the only or the ideal development.

Jung also posits a distinction between the causes of dictator-ship and those factors that engender communism. Dictatorship results from the *social atomization of individuals,* which leads to their banding together in groups and organizations that then serve to extinguish individual personality and responsibility. Communism, he implies, is the result of the individuals' *total dependence upon the state,* of their demand that the state satis-fy all their material wants. Thus a dictatorship is obviously pos-sible without communism: any atomized and deindividualized grouping is open to dictatorship; as long as the individuals do not look to the state to satisfy their material, and perhaps other needs, communism will not arise. On the other hand, commu-nism seems impossible to Jung without dictatorship, since it rests on and very often, in order to preserve itself, fosters the iso-lation, disorganization, and helplessness of the individual. Al-though the noncommunist dictator might have greater scope for the imposition of his personal *will* upon the society, the com-munist dictator, once he accepts certain ideological and eco-nomic limitations, has greater personal *power:* for the former, the demands of his subjects are not necessarily ideological and are certainly not economic; for the latter, the demands encom-pass every conceivable human need—spiritual, social, material.

Jung argues further that a welfare society composed of dein-dividualized human beings with an undeveloped sense of indi-vidual responsibility for self-preservation and morality is com-pletely at the mercy of anyone who manages to get into one of the offices that allows him to manipulate state policy. Such a person is the only one in the society who can make use of his individuality, provided he is strong enough to separate himself from the official state ideology, and he is then subject to no higher authority. In the communist state, however, the men in power are usually servants of the official ideology and attitudes and are just as much social units as the ruled. They are merely distinguished "by the fact that they are specialized mouthpieces of the State doctrine. They do not need to be personalities capable of judgment, but thoroughgoing specialists who are unusable outside their line of business."[11]

The history of the communist countries is instructive in this respect. It seems that a strong personality, whose will is law and whose ideas become the official ideology, has been necessary for the founding of these states. Once the state is firmly established and the leader dies, the "cult of personality" is denounced, and "collective leadership" takes over. The new leaders merely satisfy the expectations of the collective ruling elite and the ideology; they are bureaucrats and ideological mouthpieces, and displays of individuality or personality on their part is frowned on.

Thus the historical, cultural, and economic developments of the past four centuries, which began as movements for individual dignity and freedom, have paradoxically led to the destruction of individuality. What is more, even the remedies that the individual has sought for this condition have turned against him.[12] He has been dispersed, isolated, and made an insignificant member of a mass: to combat his isolation he organizes, and the organization then perpetuates his isolation and procedurally reinforces his insignificance. His material livelihood has been disrupted and his survival threatened: to protect himself he demands a social welfare system, which then divests him of all responsibility and turns him into a helpless and dependent creature totally at the mercy of the administrators of the system. He has been rendered powerless and politically inefficacious: to

11. *Ibid.*, pp. 252–53.
12. In the *Critique de la Raison Dialectique*, Sartre calls this perverse yet apparently inevitable historical phenomenon the "anti-dialectic."

satisfy his will to power, he supports an absolute state, which then terrorizes him and makes certain that he will not have any power or political efficacy at all. Finally, his obedience to the Church and his religious beliefs have been undermined: since he must have faith, he transfers his allegiance to the state, which then makes use of his need to believe in something beyond himself to augment its hold over him.

Jung maintains that the communist or fascist state's absorption of man's religious feelings is one of the advantages that such a state possesses over the secular democratic one. He insists that "religion, in the sense of conscientious regard for the irrational factors of the psyche and individual fate," or "as the careful observation and taking account of certain invisible and uncontrollable factors, is an *instinctive* attitude peculiar to man."[13] Its manifestations, traceable through all human history, may vary, but the instinct is always present. The rationalistic and so-called "enlightened" critique of religious doctrines and contents misses the point: it does not and cannot affect the psychological function that is the foundation of religious beliefs. Being deprived of one set of gods, mankind will only create others. Therefore, given the modern antireligious bias together with the elevation of the state to the supreme principle, the religious function often reappears in the deification of the state. The state simply takes the place of God; "that is why, seen from this angle, the socialist [or fascist] dictatorships are religions and State slavery is a form of worship."[14] Without too great an effort, the state obtains the same uncritical enthusiasm, self-sacrifice, and love that were formerly bestowed upon the Church. Thus, "National Socialism," Jung observes, "comes as near to being a religious movement as any movement since A.D. 622," while "com-

13. *The Undiscovered Self*, volume 10, pp. 261 and 259.
14. *Ibid.*, p. 259.

munism claims to be paradise come to earth again."[15] It also follows that, as with religious devotees, rational or empirical criticism of nationalist or socialist ideologies will have little or no effect upon their adherents. No doubt writing in a somewhat wry vein, Jung also notes that to the extent that religion "requires or presupposes the 'fear of God,' then the dictator State takes good care to provide the necessary terror."[16]

Jung enumerates the major parallels between the modern secular and the earlier religious beliefs. He writes that "the goals of religion—deliverance from evil, reconciliation with God, rewards in the hereafter, and so on—turn into worldly promises about freedom from care for one's daily bread, the just distribution of material goods, universal prosperity in the future, and shorter working hours."[17] The fact that the fulfillment of these promises is always as near, and as far off, as paradise only furnishes another analogy. Instead of religious processions, rituals, invocations, icons, statues, and fireworks to scare off demons, there are military parades, state ceremonies, official speeches, portraits, busts, and "spontaneous" mass demonstrations to instill fear into the state's enemies. However, Jung thinks that there is a vital difference between the "suggestive parade of State power" and the various religious gatherings. Both engender a feeling of collective security, but the secular demonstrations deal primarily with external events and give the individual no protection against inner demons, inner fears. Hence he clings "all the more to the power of the State, i.e., to the mass, thus delivering himself up to it psychologically as well as morally and putting the finishing touch to his social depotentation."[18]

15. "Psychological Commentary on 'The Tibetan Book of the Great Liberation,' " volume 11, p. 488.
16. *The Undiscovered Self,* volume 10, p. 260.
17. *Ibid.*
18. *Ibid.*

Still, in the end, Jung believes, the religious function cannot be perverted in this manner permanently. In time, doubts arise in the individual. In most cases these are immediately repressed because of the fear of opposing the general trend and the official doctrine. The doubts then lead to overcompensation in the form of fanaticism with the repression of the doubts supplying the psychic energy. The fanaticism, in turn, is used to stamp out any opposition or divergence of opinion, both in the fanatic and in others: "The policy of the State is exalted to a creed, the leader or party boss becomes a demigod beyond good and evil, and his votaries are honoured as heroes, martyrs, apostles, missionaries. There is only *one* truth and beside it no other. It is sacrosanct and above criticism. Anyone who thinks differently is a heretic, who, as we know from history, is threatened with all manner of unpleasant things. Only the party boss, who holds the political power in his hands, can interpret the State doctrine authentically, and he does so just as suits him."[19] Of course, doubt, heresy, and fanticism are not new, nor are they confined to secular ideologies. But the dislocation of the religious function into the secular realm, its serious distortion, as well as the absolute state's insistence on unquestioning adherence to the official ideology all work to produce greater doubt and resistance than is normally the case with a religious movement. The greater doubt and resistance then lead to a more intense propaganda, fanatacism, and so on.

Thus, in Jung's view, "slavery and rebellion are inseparable correlates," and any inordinate concentration of power gives rise to "unconscious subversive tendencies."[20] The greater the power, the stronger these tendencies, which are then manifested in a rivalry for power and in an exaggerated distrust or paranoia

19. *Ibid.,* p. 259.
20. *Ibid.,* p. 253.

that pervades the entire political and social system. Then, in order to disguise subversive tendencies and to protect himself in a hostile world, the individual adopts hypocrisy as his modus vivendi.

A totalitarian state, therefore, always lives on the brink of rebellion. Its extreme power calls forth an equally extreme resistance. A totalitarian regime is not wrong in sensing that the majority of its subjects are opposed to it. From its vantage point, the constant vigilance of the secret police over the populace is fully justified. Moreover, the regime must be ready to use its power at the slightest provocation, for once the rebellion starts there may be no controlling it. Liberalization in a totalitarian or absolute state is always fraught with dangers and seldom successful. There are no intermediate corporate bodies between the state and the individual, and once the state relinquishes some of its prerogatives they are taken up in a spontaneous and unorganized way and frequently directed against the powers of the state. Hence there is a temptation to revert to the earlier absolute control rather than risk anarchy, or, in time, organized resistance. The "tightening up" that followed the Soviet liberalization after Stalin's death, and the invasion of Czechoslovakia that followed the "Prague Spring" of 1968, can be seen as illustrative of this principle. Thus, as a rule, an absolute or a totalitarian state must continue to exist with all its powers intact or be completely overthrown, for it is not amenable to gradual reform.

Because the concept of "community" is an indispensable aid for the organization of any disparate group of individuals, the modern dictatorial state, like the Church in earlier times, lays great emphasis on this ideal. In fact, "community" or "society" is the central concern of communism and socialism, as their etymologies indicate. But since the ideal is "thrust down the throats of the people so much," the effort to inculcate a "sense

of community" more often than not inspires divisive mistrust.[21]
Moreover, Jung thinks that the communal ideal, by stressing the
collective and social qualities of the individual, puts a premium
on the lowest common denominator, on mediocrity, and "on
everything that settles down to vegetate in an easy, irresponsible
way."[22] Thus, in spite of the announced ennobling aims of socialism and communism, they lower the level of culture by restricting and inhibiting the possibilities of individual development.
Moreover, the larger and more closely knit the community, the
greater the sum of the collective forces detrimental to individual
expression and development. In any tightly knit community,
whether large or small, and no matter how idealistic its aims, the
individual is "morally and spiritually crushed, and, as a result,
the one source of moral and spiritual progress for society is
choked up."[23]

Together with the notion of community, modern social movements also stress the ideal of equality. Jung agrees that equality
before the law is a salutary principle, but he thinks less of equality when it is applied to every other sphere of social life, particularly on the assumption that uniform regulations and egali-
tarian reforms "would automatically ensure a uniform distribution of happiness."[24] It is a delusion to imagine that equality of
income or equal opportunities would have the same value for
everyone. Jung speaks of these matters in the Epilogue to his
book on *Psychological Types,* where he confronts the fact of the
heterogeneity of men in the ways they experience and valuate the
world. On the basis of his studies, he argues that the requirements for happiness and well-being are so different among indi-

21. *Ibid.,* p. 261.
22. *Two Essays,* volume 7, p. 150, and "A Study in the Process of Individuation,"
volume 9, part 1, p. 349.
23. *Two Essays,* volume 7, p. 150.
24. *Psychological Types,* volume 6, p. 487.

viduals that no legislation could ever approximate and do justice to them all. Nor can social legislation ever overcome the fundamental psychological differences among the various personality types; in fact, this would not be desirable, for the interplay of the differences generates the creative and vital energy of society.

Jung is firmly convinced that the individual is "the sole carrier of mind and life,"[25] and that "all the highest achievements of virtue, as well as the blackest villainies, are individual."[26] In a collective society, however, both the virtues and the vices of the individual are ascribed to the community as a whole; and since, in fact, the mass-minded and the mass-organized community has seriously restricted the individual's personal and moral development, there is some truth to this ascription. Under such conditions, the often quoted Marxist thesis that in essence the individual is only the "ensemble of his social relations" is a self-validating statement. But the "communization" or the "socialization" of the individual is not accomplished without serious psychological and social repercussions. For the various individualistic elements of the psyche that are not accorded a useful and healthy outlet are repressed and fall into the unconscious where they are "transformed into something essentially baleful, destructive, and anarchical."[27] Internally, they give rise to personal neuroses and psychoses; externally, their malevolent force may appear in spectacular crimes—assassinations, for example. In most people, however, the repressed energy "remains in the background, and only manifests itself indirectly in the inexorable moral degeneration of society."[28] When the problems reach intolerable proportions, more collective measures are called for to combat these anarchistic and demoralizing forces—the

25. "The Fight with the Shadow," volume 10, p. 225.
26. *Two Essays,* volume 7, p. 150.
27. *Ibid.*
28. *Ibid.*

various "wars" on drug addiction, crime, official corruption, and so on. But it is foolish and hopeless, Jung asserts, to stake everything on collective programs and procedures, for, in the end, the nature of the collective "depends on the spiritual and moral stature of the individuals composing it."[29] And in the modern state, the individuals making up the collective are in a demoralized and spiritually atrophied condition. The only way to cure the general ill is through appropriate changes in the individual. But just as masses cannot be changed through collective efforts, neither can fundamental changes in the individual be brought about through "communistic or Christian baptisms *en masse,* which do not touch the inner man."[30]

All basic changes in the individual are the culmination of a natural process that begins with the personal encounter between man and man, and between the individual and his God. Jung insists that the only effective counterbalance to mass-mindedness, to the deindividualizing influence of the collective, and to the demoralizing effects of the dictatorial state is an individual inner transcendent experience. Only on the basis of such an experience can the individual resist the moral blandishments of the world and protect himself from an otherwise inevitable submersion in the mass. "Intellectual or even moral insight into the stultification and moral irresponsibility of the mass man is a negative recognition only."[31] Such insight is wavering in resolve and passive in its effects: "it lacks the driving force of religious conviction."[32] The "confessions" of many prominent Soviet Communists during the Moscow Trials of the 1930s are an example of the psychic bankruptcy of collectively oriented individuals when

29. "A Study in the Process of Individuation," volume 9, part 1, p. 349, and *The Undiscovered Self,* volume 10, p. 261.
30. *The Undiscovered Self,* volume 10, p. 262.
31. *Ibid.,* p. 258.
32. *Ibid.,* pp. 258–59.

faced with an ideology, the political power of the state, and arguments of *raison d'état*. The cerebral ruminations involved in such "confessions" are dramatically documented in Arthur Koestler's *Darkness at Noon*. The cases of Jean-Paul Sartre and Albert Camus are also instructive. As existentialists, both stressed the priority of the individual. But Sartre, the atheistic rationalist, capitulated to the intellectual and political logic of Marxist Communism and hence "abandoned" the individual. The more pantheistic, moralistic Camus withstood the temptation of communism and insisted on an unconditional separation between the individual and the state—his ethic of permanent rebellion.[33]

Finally, Jung concludes that *"resistance to the organized mass can be effected only by the man who is as well organized in his individuality as the mass itself."*[34] Unfortunately, this proposition is, in Jung's opinion, unintelligible to contemporary men, since it requires that the individual recognize, understand, and attempt to master the forces of his unconscious. But until the individual does realize and undertake these tasks, he will continue to be vulnerable to mass movements, mesmerized by powerful "leaders," and serve as a pawn in little understood political and social upheavals.

Jung does not develop the theme, but one of the most common problems in the relationship between the individual and the state is the individual's projection of the father or mother imago onto the state.[35] Patriotism should be the conscious appreciation of

33. For a more detailed discussion of the relation between Sartre, Camus, and Communism, see my *Marxism and Existentialism* (New York: Anchor Books, 1965).

34. *The Undiscovered Self*, volume 10, p. 278.

35. An excellent documented study of such projections is Hans Marti's *Urbild und Verfassung* (Bern and Stuttgart: Verlag Hans Huber, n.d.). Marti traces the change of the archetypal images and values underlying the Swiss Constitution from the original patriarchal *Männerbund* and *Vaterland* to the current maternal conception of *Helvetia Mater* and *Heimat*.

one's history and culture; the attribution of fatherhood or motherhood to a state or to a particular regime, and the child-like awe, respect, and obedience that follow are immature per-versions of the patriotic ideal. Under such conditions individual responsibility and development cease.

Another form of this projection is the use of the social struc-ture or the state as a substitute object for antiparental disobedi-ence and rebellion.[36] The student rebellions of the late 1960s involved a good dose of this projected generational conflict. The reasons vary, but the fact is that for many student rebels the home was not an appropriate place to engage in the normal struggle against parental authority and for personal freedom.[37] Consequently, the university, the social structure, and the state bore the brunt of their adolescent rebellion, with its search for "reality," limits, personal identity, and responsibility. But where individual responsibility, in this case parental responsibility, is abandoned or abrogated to the society and the state, the process of individual maturation will also take on a collective form—and will be dealt with in an impersonal, collective way.

Another "perversion" of the individual's relationship with the state involves the projection of his personal responsibility onto the society or the state. In this instance, personal responsibility is not relinquished because of a projection of the parental image. Instead there is a failure to take it up, partly because of the human tendency to take the easiest course, and partly because of the immensity and complexity of the problems that individuals

36. It should be noted that chronological maturity is no protection against either form of the projection of the parental imago.

37. For an excellent 1967 "case-study" whose major hypotheses were borne out by future events and later studies, see Richard Flacks, "The Liberated Generation: An Ex-ploration of the Roots of Student Protest" in F. I. Greenstein and M. Lerner, eds., *A Source Book for the Study of Personality and Politics* (Chicago: Markham Publishing Co., Inc., 1971). See also, Lewis Feuer, *The Conflict of Generations: The Character and Significance of Student Movements* (New York: Basic Books, 1969).

face in contemporary society. The state is often left with no option except to take over responsibility in more and more areas because individuals do not feel themselves capable of dealing with the multitude of problems confronting them. The disintegration of traditional communities, urbanization, social mobility, and the resulting atomization and isolation of individuals all tend to produce this despondent attitude. Furthermore, the centralization and growth of bureaucracy that result when the state assumes "parental" responsibility make it almost impossible, even for a willing citizen, to be aware of and feel responsible for the developments and policies that occur in his name. Withdrawal and apathy may follow, or the sense of helplessness may be compensated for by an identification with the power of the state—a particularly dangerous form of psychic inflation.

Given Jung's appreciation for the creative powers of the collective unconscious, it might at first seem strange for him to place such overriding emphasis on the individual. Indeed, his statements that the individual is the "sole carrier of mind and life," the one source of moral and spiritual progress, and the fountainhead of the "highest achievements of virtue as well as the blackest of villainies," may seem to smack either of paradox or rhetorical exaggeration. But these statements cannot be taken in isolation from Jung's psychological theories. In their proper context, what they connote is that the various aspects of the collective unconscious make their appearance and are realized only through individuals. The individual alone is capable of embodying and consciously applying the energy of the unconscious. Where there is no individual consciousness and responsibility, the archetypes operate of their own accord, using groups and individuals as their instruments. And since they contain both positive and negative, creative and destructive forces, and hardly discriminate between the two, without the individual's conscious intervention they operate like all natural forces—with no regard for human needs or morality.

Underlying many of Jung's arguments, including his treatment of surplus psychic energy, of consciousness and the unconscious, of positive and negative psychic inflation, of individualism and collectivism, of fanaticism and scepticism, of power and rebellion, it is possible to discern basic principles involving the interplay of opposites in complex relationships. There is, for example, the tension between opposites that is the source of psychic energy. Opposites "strive" to attain a balance, or homeostasis; there is the possibility of the synthesis or union of opposites. There is the concept of the conversion of an extreme element into its opposite, a process that Jung calls *enantiodromia*. And frequently there is a compensatory relationship between opposites, as in the case of external compensation for neglected inner psychic needs through the "externalization" of repressed psychic contents. Thus, where there is psychological insecurity, anxiety, and fear, there will arise demands for security, order, and force. Where there exists a feeling of individual weakness and worthlessness, there will be a demand for collective power and pride. Where there is no self-certainty or self-knowledge, there will be calls for more education, scientific research, and authority. Where there is no individual self-identity, it will be sought in group identity. Where the individual has no personal faith and his religious feelings are neglected, a collective devotion to secular movements and ideologies will take their place. When the emotions and the unconscious are starved for individual experiences befitting their needs, there will arise demands on the society to provide a variety of material and emotional satisfactions. Where there is discomfort and pain in the psyche, a search will be made for external comfort and pleasure. When the individual does not feel psychologically healthy, he will project and blame his illness on society and insist that it improve itself, or at least treat him. Where the irrational, primitive, violent drives of the individual's psyche are denied and repressed, they will appear in mass immorality, corruption, and crime. And when the individual's psyche is at war with itself, class, racial, and national wars will follow. In other words, there is a kind of symbiosis between internal, psychological forces and those of the external environment. The situation is "infectious," affecting everyone, and like the self-devouring Ouroboros the world rolls ever closer to suicide. Jung would probably claim that much of the convulsive history of the twentieth century is directly traceable to various expressions of pressures such as these. Unfortunately, he believes that the reactions are natural, and, in the light of past developments, almost inevitable. The individual and the society are caught up in the interplay of opposites. Just as primitive men externalized their inner psychological drives onto objects and movements in nature, so contemporary men externalize their psychological drives onto society and politics. Up to a point, the externalization is therapeutic and palliative of the more extreme symptoms of the psychological problems of the modern individual. But it is dangerous, for it is palliative only at the expense of the individual's relinquishing his responsibility for his destiny to the "gods" that he has created.

In the end, compensatory externalization merely postpones the necessary "operation," for no amount of maneuvering of external conditions will cure the basic psychological disease. Jung insists that if the problems confronting modern man are to be solved, the externalization must cease, the projections must be withdrawn, and the individual must come face to face with his self, particularly with the still unknown, primitive forces of his unconscious. Only then can he begin to make a valid distinction between the problems that are soluble externally, or socially, and those that are only soluble internally, or psychologically, and not confuse the two. With the resulting increase in consciousness and knowledge, man could begin to create his individual destiny, determine the nature of his society, and shape his history, instead of being threatened with destruction by the interplay of natural forces which he does not understand and over which he has no control.

5

Politics and the Unconscious

The most significant problem of modern man consists in his resisting the temptation to lose his individuality in a mass society and in preventing the emergence of a highly centralized, all-powerful state. These eventualities, Jung asserts, can be avoided only through a conscious effort directed toward the development of individual awareness, moral self-reliance, and psychological self-knowledge. Such development cannot occur without an appreciation of the intimate bond between the individual and his society, and particularly, without insight into the effects of the unconscious on politics.

To begin with—and contrary to the spirit of the times—the individual must recognize that he is, in fact, the pivot around which consciousness, society, and history develop. Nothing can occur without the participation of individuals, whether conscious or unconscious. And if both individuality itself and society are threatened with chaos and extinction, it is a result, in the last analysis, of the weakness or blindness of individuals. By the same token, the individual alone is capable of recognizing the problem and altering the situation.

Jung is adamant about this premise, even to the point of claiming that a society or a state derives its quality from the mental condition of the individuals composing it. Therefore, if there exists worldwide confusion and disorder, it must, he asserts, "reflect a similar condition in the mind of the individual."[1] And if a movement grips an entire nation, it must have struck a sympathetic chord in every individual as well. Moreover, each individual is a "cell in the structure of various international organisms and is...causally implicated in their conflicts."[2] Even though the individual may often feel consciously that he is more or less meaningless and the victim of uncontrollable forces, in fact, he "harbours within himself a dangerous shadow and adversary who is involved as an invisible helper in the dark machinations of the political monster."[3]

The difficulty, however, is that the individual is not aware of these facts, and the sociologically oriented ideological propositions of the day conceal them from him. He simply does not fathom the fundamental role he plays in the formation of the social and political movements around him. It is somewhat perplexing and ironic that despite the findings of the science of psychology, modern man continues to think and act as if he were *"simplex* and not *duplex."*[4] He still identifies himself with the fictitious picture of man drawn by Enlightenment rationalism, which assumes the psyche is a tabula rasa at birth, and that with the appropriate environment and education, men are basically innocent, reasonable, and good.

Unfortunately, this view and the cultural-social practices resulting from it fail to provide an outlet for the irrational and primitive impulses of the psyche. The resulting neglect and

1. "The Fight with the Shadow," volume 10, p. 221.
2. *The Undiscovered Self,* volume 10, p. 299.
3. *Ibid.*
4. *Ibid.,* p. 290.

repression intensify and distort these impulses, and where they could have been expressed in a personal and controllable manner, they sink to the level of the collective unconscious and then emerge in tempestuous mass psychoses and movements. Under such circumstances, the observation is valid that "it is not the will of individuals that moulds the destinies of nations, but suprapersonal factors."[5] And so, although today Western man is no longer at the mercy of wild beasts and the elements of nature, he is still battered by the forces of his own psyche: "This is the World Power that vastly exceeds all other powers on earth."[6]

These enormously powerful and yet generally unrecognized psychic forces engender the delusive social and political systems described in the previous chapter, which are not merely the necessary consequences of external conditions, but developments precipitated by the collective unconscious. And so long as external and psychological conditions remain as they are today, there is always the danger that "at any moment several millions of human beings may be smitten with a new madness, and then we shall have another world war or devastating revolution."[7] Or being spared that, all that is needed is "an almost imperceptible disturbance of equilibrium in a few of our rulers' heads to plunge the world into blood, fire, and radioactivity."[8]

Thus, if for no other reason than survival, the individual today is forced to examine and learn to deal with the personal and collective powers of his unconscious. The first task is to become aware of his *shadow*. The shadow is the other side of the con-

5. "The Swiss Line in the European Spectrum," volume 10, p. 487. Instead of "gods" or "fate," the controlling elements are now called "factors." And in the realm of consciousness, it is assumed that men themselves compose the various factors, and that, therefore, with enough knowledge, power, and good will, the factors should be amenable to control.
6. "Epilogue to *Essays on Contemporary Events,*" volume 10, p. 235.
7. *Ibid.*
8. *The Undiscovered Self,* volume 10, p. 291.

scious personality. It is the unrecognized, incompatible, and inferior part of the personality—"the sum of all those unpleasant qualities we like to hide, together with the insufficiently developed functions and contents of the personal unconscious."[9] And since the unconscious, like the conscious, is both personal and collective, there also exists a *collective shadow*—the unrecognized, incompatible, and inferior side of a race, group, or nation. Because the shadow, whether personal or collective, contains all those aspects of the psyche which consciousness does not want to recognize, it is usually effectively repressed. Yet the more it is repressed, the more it is deprived of conscious or social expression, the larger and darker it grows. For despite all its unpleasant and negative characteristics, it is a living part of the psyche and requires some form of affirmation. It will not be argued out of existence or rationalized into harmlessness. Nor would that be desirable, even if it were possible, for without the shadow, the personality is a plastic, two-dimensional phantom—it lacks depth. A man who is unaware of his negative or evil side is like a well-mannered child: his conscious and moral development are incomplete. By not bringing the repressed contents of his shadow to consciousness, which would produce a tension of opposites and a degree of disaffection with his being, man deprives himself of the possibility for further progress in the development of his psyche.

Unfortunately, the "man without a shadow" is statistically the commonest human type, one who imagines that "he actually *is* only what he cares to know about himself,...[and] neither the so-called religious man nor the man of scientific pretensions

9. *Two Essays,* volume 7, n. 5, p. 65. Elsewhere, Jung writes that he could easily have coined "a less 'poetic' and more scientific-looking Greco-Latin neologism," but he feels that the "shadow," with its literary and emotional connotations, its flexibility, is more appropriate; he finds even the phrase "the inferior part of the personality" inadequate and misleading ("On the Nature of the Psyche," volume 8, p. 208).

forms any exception to this rule."[10] Such men possess no "imagination for evil" and consequently no sense of guilt. They have the dubious and, in fact, unwarranted "privilege of being at all times 'not guilty' of the social and political catastrophes in which the whole world is engulfed."[11] They are not responsible for anything and never make mistakes; for them the only thing that makes mistakes is that anonymous collectivity known as "Society" or the "State." Such blindness to the evil present within man is both foolish and harmful: foolish because only the fool can disregard the conditions of his own nature; and harmful because "it deprives us of the *capacity to deal with evil.*"[12] For the fact is that much of human history is a record of the evil and injustice that men have inflicted upon other men. When one reflects upon man's deeds, the evil that comes to light, and which undoubtedly dwells within him, is of such gigantic proportions "that for the Church to talk of original sin and to trace it back to Adam's relatively innocent slipup with Eve is almost a euphemism. The case is far graver and is grossly underestimated."[13] And although man may not deny the terrible things that have happened and still go on happening, he always insists it is "the others" who do them. In reality he should recognize that since we all share in the same human nature, we bear within us the capacity and the inclination to do all the acts that were done by others. Although juridically we may be innocent, in fact, because of our human nature we are all potential criminals; frequently, the opportunity merely has not presented itself. And "whether the crime occurred many generations back or happens today, it remains the symptom of a disposition that is always and everywhere present. ...None of us stands outside

10. "On the Nature of the Psyche," volume 8, p. 208.
11. *Ibid.,* p. 209.
12. *The Undiscovered Self,* volume 10, p. 297.
13. *Ibid.,* p. 296.

humanity's black collective shadow."[14]

Thus, the "realization of the shadow," which for modern man includes the realization of the evil within his own nature, is not only an intellectual, but also an ethical problem. And, while it may seem to be purely a question of personal psychic development, in reality it is, at the same time, a social matter; once the individual recognizes the role that his unconscious plays in social and political processes, he feels the responsibility for his psychic constitution and health even more keenly.

The fact that the shadow contains the weaknesses and the inadequacies of the psyche should in no way be taken to mean that it is weak and powerless. On the contrary, as reflection on man's capacity for evil reveals, it is charged with a "positively demonic dynamism."[15] This is especially the case where it has been intensely repressed, but even without repression it possesses a power of its own. For the shadow was originally a collective aspect of the psyche and still functions autonomously. Its collective representations or projections can be traced in such fairy-tale figures as Tom Thumb or Stupid Hans, and in various folk characters and customs: the medieval Fools' Feasts, for example, with their ribaldry and parodies of officialdom, including the election of Fools' bishops or popes; the American Indian Winnebago Trickster figure; and the modern clown. The motifs of collective representations of the shadow include reversal of hierarchic order; fondness for sly jokes and malicious pranks; duality of nature—half-animal, half-divine; ability to alter shape; exposure to ridicule and torture; associations with healing; and intimations of salvation.[16]

The collective representation of the shadow breaks up under

14. *Ibid.*, p. 297.
15. *Two Essays*, volume 7, p. 29.
16. "On the Psychology of the Trickster-Figure," volume 9, part 1, p. 255.

the impact of civilization and the growing differentiation of individual consciousness, and its chief characteristics become personalized and thereby made subject to individual responsibility. But the personalization of the collective shadow is a relatively recent development; regression to its collective form easily occurs whenever the individual is submerged in a mass, as recent European history has shown, and in this form it can even become incarnate in a specific man or group. On the biological level, union with the shadow is "obedience to instinct," and on the psychological level, identification with the shadow results in psychic inflation. The combination produces such a sense of dynamic energy and power that the individual or group feels superhuman, godlike, and, like Zarathustra, "six thousand feet beyond good and evil."[17] On the other hand, the uncovering of the primitive brutality and force of the shadow may also lead to physical lethargy and a psychological sense of unworthiness and powerlessness, as was pointed out in the discussion of psychic inflation.

Unconscious and repressed contents of the psyche readily lend themselves to projection. Projections may be positive or negative and may be defined as the erroneous attribution of an individual's or a group's unconscious qualities to the environment or to another individual or group. Particularly, negative projections serve as defense mechanisms that help an individual or a group avoid facing the incompatible and disturbing contents of the psyche. Such externalization of inner feeling-conflicts is one avenue by which the shadow is able to find an outward and socially acceptable expression, and both positive and negative projections play a vital role in politics. Most probably because of the feeling for self-preservation, negative projections choose objects at a distance, while favorable projections settle upon objects

17. *Two Essays*, volume 7, p. 31.

close at hand.[18]

Because of their unconscious nature, projections are usually naive in form and thoroughly undiscriminating. War psychology and chauvinism are ideal examples: everything my country does is good, while everything the others do is bad. Similarly, during the "cold war" it "became a political and social duty to apostrophize the capitalism of the one [side] and the communism of the other as the very devil."[19] The shadow, therefore, is invariably projected onto "others," and in politics, the "others" are one's political enemies. Since the negative projection carries with it "the *fear* which we involuntarily and secretly feel for our own evil over to the other side," it increases the formidableness of the threat.[20] A consideration of the psychological process taking place discloses that the projection really reveals our own unconscious characteristics: "We simply accuse our enemy of our own unadmitted faults."[21] The very judgment we pronounce upon our enemy, we, in fact, pronounce upon an unconscious part of ourselves. We rage against an unrecognized component of our own being. Indeed, one of the ways to recognize a negative projection and learn to know our shadow is to pay attention exactly to those people and situations that arouse in us intense discomfort, animosity, and hatred.

A complication of the phenomenon of projection results from the fact that "*all projections provoke counter-projections* when the object is unconscious of the quality projected upon it by the subject."[22] Frequently the object may offer a "hook" to the pro-

18. The neurotic forms an exception to this rule: "He has such an intensive relationship to his immediate surroundings that he cannot prevent even the unfavorable projections from flowing into the objects closest to him and arousing conflicts" ("General Aspects of Dream Psychology," volume 8, p. 271).

19. *The Undiscovered Self,* volume 10, pp. 280–81.

20. *Ibid.,* p. 297.

21. "General Aspects of Dream Psychology," volume 8, p. 270.

22. *Ibid.,* p. 273.

jection and even "lure" it out. This particularly is the case where the person who is the object is "not conscious of the quality in question: in that way it works directly upon the unconscious of the projicient."[23] In this manner, a compulsive, "mystical" or unconscious identity is established between the projicient and the receiver of the projection. They become "one soul" and seem to need each other for their psychic existence and balance, even though in the process they may be destroying each other. At the same time, there always arise resistances against such unconscious ties—conscious resistances, "if the subject's attitude allows him to give his libido only voluntarily, but not to have it coaxed or forced out of him; unconscious resistances if he likes nothing better than having his libido taken away from him."[24]

Because these psychic interactions are complex, the emotions, conflicts, and events they engender are only dimly understood and appear to occur "of their own accord." A note of fatalism thus enters human relations, which is dangerous in politics, where these emotions and conflicts are magnified in power and in scope. Projections perpetuate man's blindness concerning the unconscious and its influence upon social and political relations. Unfortunately, however, things are further complicated by the fact that, from a purely psychological standpoint, it is hardly desirable to avoid projections at all costs. Becoming too conscious of our projections, for instance, "may easily act as an impediment to our relations with others, for there is then no bridge of illusion across which love and hate can stream off so relievingly."[25] The libido is "dammed up," the negative elements of the unconscious gain in energy and force their way to consciousness. Even negative projections serve a useful purpose, for without them "the individual is then faced with the task of putting

23. *Ibid.*
24. *Ibid.*
25. *Ibid.*, p. 272.

down to his own account all the iniquity, devilry, etc., which he has blandly attributed to others and about which he has been indignant all his life."[26] This may be so demoralizing and destructive to an individual's or a group's ego-image that the psyche may again repress the unfavorable elements and once more displace them onto external objects. "The real existence of an enemy upon whom one can foist off everything evil," including all one's ambitions for reeducation and improvement is an enormous relief for one's conscience and for the compensating sense of idealism.[27] "You can then at least say, without hesitation, who the devil is; you are quite certain that the cause of your misfortune is outside and not in your own attitude."[28] Thus do "normal" people act out their mental disturbances and protect themselves from the shadow aspects of their psyches through the use of social and political forms, including wars and revolutions.[29]

The psyche, therefore, needs and even helps to create the enemy. Since its projections are answered in kind, it never fails to succeed in its intent. And then it has the objectively evident enmity of the enemy to justify its own antagonistic feelings. In some ways, the psyche's victory would be complete were it not for the actual threat that the enemy then poses to the individual's well-being or survival. Where the disturbances of the psyche are especially severe, it is possible that it may be deliberately courting its own destruction by creating real enemies. This self-destructiveness is particularly apparent in the neurotic or psychotic individual, but it is also true of groups. Indeed, Jung maintains that because of the post-Enlightenment repression

26. *Ibid.*
27. *Ibid.*
28. *Ibid.*
29. Only the neurotic cannot avoid dealing with the negative contents of the unconscious in a personal way.

of the unconscious and of the shadow components of the psyche, Western civilization as a whole suffers from a severe neurosis which makes its presence felt in modern political conflicts and in the toying with self-annihilation represented by the atomic arms race, for example.

Thus Jung believes that, while in a fairly balanced individual or group psyche negative projections are useful, in a psyche in which the shadow is strongly repressed they become dangerous. For the severe repression of the shadow energizes the negative contents of the unconscious and actually forces their projection onto objects outside the individual or group involved. Thus is produced a neurotic, and sometimes psychotic, personality or society, with its compulsive search for conflict and self-destruction. A certain amount of consciousness and acceptance of the shadow helps avoid this potentially dangerous development. It checks the projection of the psyche's negative qualities upon others and the involuntary need for and creation of enemies, and it promotes a degree of modesty and humility and an increased sense of personal responsibility for the social and political problems of the world. For "nothing has a more divisive and alienating effect upon society than... moral complacency and lack of responsibility, and nothing promotes understanding and *rapprochement* more than the mutual withdrawal of projections."[30] Obviously, for these developments to take place, first self-knowledge and then self-criticism on the part of individuals are necessary. Once men are taught to look at the lowly side of their nature, Jung writes, they may also learn to understand and to love their fellow man better. "A little less hypocrisy and a little more tolerance towards oneself can only have good results in respect for our neighbour; for we are all too prone to transfer to our fellows the injustice and violence we inflict upon our own

30. *The Undiscovered Self*, volume 10, pp. 299–300.

natures."[31] Both in the history of the collective and of the individual everything, therefore, depends on the development of consciousness. That alone can bring liberation from the unconscious. Jung notes that at the end of the trickster myth, the unconscious collective shadow externalized in that myth intimates the possibility of salvation from the calamities that the shadow perpetrates against humanity. And he concludes on the optimistic note that, both in its collective and in its individual form, the shadow also "contains within it the seed of an enantiodromia, of a conversion into its opposite."[32]

As long as men remain unconscious of their personal and collective shadow, they will always need and make enemies. This premise has special significance for politics. It is remarkable, for example, to observe how the political enemies of yesterday, who only recently were maligned in the press and regarded by the public as the very incarnation of evil, become the allies of today and suddenly turn out to be quite human and even charming. The names change—from German to Russian, from Japanese to Chinese, to mention a few of the recent American obsessions—but the reactions remain the same and are always total: enemies are to be despised, allies loved or respected, and any feelings to the contrary are treasonous or subversive. This all-or-nothing response is particularly true of the mass man, who cannot tolerate ambiguity. The psychologically undifferentiated individual is seized by a psychopolitical stream of events over which he has no control. Every successful dictator and even politician is aware of this response and manipulates it to further his or his party's political ends. Moreover, the enemy does not have to be foreign:

31. *Two Essays,* volume 7, p. 262.
32. "On the Psychology of the Trickster-Figure," volume 9, part 1, p. 272.

Jews, Communists, the bourgeoisie, blacks, whites are equally useful and can engender the same unequivocal response in the mass. For in addition to political enemies, people tend to project their shadow onto anyone who is different or distant from them. The lower classes, or racial and national minorities serve as convenient targets for both the personal and the collective shadow projections of the dominant class and culture.

Frantz Fanon, the French-educated black psychiatrist who served in Algeria, documents the dynamics of this process under colonialism in *The Wretched of the Earth.* In a colonial society, Fanon observes, the native is regarded not only as insensible to ethics, but as the incarnation of absolute evil. "He is the corrosive element, destroying all that comes near him; he is the deforming element, disfiguring all that has to do with beauty and morality; he is the depository of maleficient powers, the unconscious and irretrievable instrument of blind forces."[33] One could hardly ask for a better definition of the shadow. And then follows the logical conclusion: the native is not human; he is a beast. Thus the settler usually refers to the native in zoological terms. "He speaks of the yellow man's reptilian motions, of the stink of the native quarter, of breeding swarms, of foulness, of spawn, of gesticulations."[34] It is no wonder that when faced with horrors that remind him of hell, the settler feels impelled to hand over the native to the Church for exorcism and purification. But not being fully convinced of the Church's power, he at the same time hedges the native in with all sorts of legal restrictions and is always prepared to use force and violence to keep him in his place. In fact, his finger is ever shaky on the trigger, for he fears the native with a fear that has more than an external basis, although he would never admit that to himself.

33. Frantz Fanon, *The Wretched of the Earth* (Baltimore: Penguin Books, 1973), p. 32.
34. *Ibid.,* p. 33.

As bad as this situation is, it is really only half the problem, for such projections have a telling effect on the psyche of those at whom they are directed. They awaken qualities in the recipient that might have lain dormant, and what is worse, they may even augment the strength of those qualities and force them to be acted out in the world. The result is, in Fanon's example, that the natives are not only forced to bear but also to act out the shadow side of the dominant culture.[35] And since the objective situation does not allow them to direct the shadow activity against the settlers, they turn it against themselves. "This is the period," Fanon continues, "when the niggers beat each other up, and the police and magistrates do not know which way to turn when faced with the astonishing waves of crime."[36] Psychic deflation, with its withdrawal, fatalism, and listlessness; semi-conscious suicide through alcohol, drugs, or individual acts of terrorism; and escape into the ecstasy of dance, music, and religion are other results of the shadow turned against one's self.

The settler, seeing the situation that has developed, now has "objective" proof that his evaluation of the native is correct, while the native develops doubts about his humanity and begins to see himself in the settler's terms. Under such conditions, the normal development of the native's personality is severly undermined. The moral, inhibitive part of his superego[37] is simply unable to cope with the collective forces that are unleashed from the unconscious, so that a general psychosis threatens. On the

35. In this regard it is interesting to note that there are statistics to show that the children of parsons in England are proportionately more in trouble with the law than children from other family backgrounds. Apparently they come under the influence of the strongly repressed shadow qualities of their parents and willy-nilly act them out.

36. Fanon, *The Wretched of the Earth*, p. 40.

37. Although Jung had strong objections to the Freudian conception of the superego and preferred to speak of conscience, he did not necessarily oppose its use as a descriptive term for the psychic functions commonly associated with conscience. I use the term in this way in these comments. See the discussion in chapter 9, pages 168 to 174, for a comparison of Freud's and Jung's conceptions of this psychic element.

other hand, the idealistic, aspirational part of the superego has no cultural models to imitate except successful native criminals or rebels, although the natives, particularly the educated class, frequently adopt the cultural ideals of the settlers—an artificial and schizophrenic result aptly described by Fanon in *Black Skin White Masks*. [38]

Finally, if and when the natives are able to turn against the settlers, it is little wonder that the long inverted shadow turns on the settlers in the same undiscriminating way in which it was projected: an enantiodromia sets in and everything connected with the settler becomes evil, and everything native good. The settler is now the devil who is to be wiped off the face of the earth, and their former oppression and degradation serve to justify the natives' attitude. To the consternation of the former

38. Frantz Fanon, *Black Skin, White Masks* (New York: Grove Press, 1967). In this book, Fanon, by way of subjecting Jung to a brief criticism, redefines the concept of collective unconscious in a way that would be unacceptable to Jung. He argues that the collective unconscious is not genetically inherited but is simply "the sum of prejudices, myths, collective attitudes of a given group," or merely "the unreflected imposition of a culture" (p. 188). He then makes use of the concept in explaining how the black, by the time he reaches maturity, is imbued with the basic attitudes of the white culture so that in his unconscious all his essential orientations are white. Consequently, he writes, it is normal for the black man to be anti-Negro. The problem is that in the collective unconscious (using Fanon's definition) of the European, the color black is identified with repressed immoral impulses. Black is the color of sin, evil, ugliness, dirt, misery, war, death. And when the European comes into contact with the black man he automatically projects all of these qualities onto him.

But Fanon thinks that these associations of the color black with various evils is specifically European and not universal. He argues that Jung's universalization of the shadow as black on the basis of the Africans he met or of the black Americans he analyzed is erroneous because all of them had suffered a more or less traumatic contact with the white man.

However, Fanon's definition of the collective unconscious is really Jung's notion of collective *consciousness,* the generally accepted and unquestioned prejudices and attitudes of a given people and period. Fanon does not really deal with Jung's view of the collective unconscious; he simply rejects it, and a redefinition is no criticism. From Jung's point of view, it is true that some of the associations with the color black are cultural, or belong to the racial or group layer of the collective unconscious. Nevertheless, he would insist that there is also a universal shadow association with black stemming from common experiences of the human race. The approach of night, for instance, has since time immemorial produced fear and search for safety. On the other hand, there are also universal associations with the color white that are similarly frightening.

masters, the listless, lazy, fatalistic native has suddenly, and for no understandable reason, become aggressive and demanding and expects "too much too soon."

Fanon's description of the colonial situation is only one illustration of the dynamics of shadow projection. To a greater or lesser extent the process is always the same, irrespective of the race, nationality, or class that happens to be the unfortunate victim of a collective shadow projection, and the end result is that extreme political actions follow what is perceived to be a threat to physical and cultural survival. This is a permanent condition under colonialism, where the settlers are greatly outnumbered by severely repressed natives; the mutual fear and distrust lead to the institutionalization of separation through policies such as apartheid, or conversely, to savage revolts like the Mau Mau movement in Kenya. In noncolonial countries, any crisis, regardless of cause, serves to strengthen shadow projections. People become agitated, insecure, angry, and quickly find someone or some group on whom to displace their discontents; strangers and minorities because helpless are useful targets. Discrimination, segregation, apartheid, anti-Semitism, national chauvinism, dogmatism, and a host of other prejudicial attitudes that attain legal or political legitimacy are thus intimately tied to and motivated by unconscious collective shadow projections.

Incidentally, collective shadow projections have a cumulative effect. They activate and support various local and personal shadow projections, so that the recipient of the collective projection is confronted by negative feelings whichever way he turns. First, the culture as a whole defines him in shadow terms; then the locality in which he lives adds its own particular flavor; and finally, each individual with whom he comes into contact contributes his own personal shadow elements. The accumulated burden is so heavy that it is not surprising that members of shadow-bearing groups are usually demoralized and depressed. Everything and everyone not only seems to be, but really is, against them. It takes a strong and unbroken cultural tradition or unusual individual self-awareness to withstand the combined onslaught.

The problems of blacks in the United States are unique in this respect. The black man's culture was almost completely destroyed by transportation and slavery, so that he had no other recourse but to adopt the cultural superego of the whites. But in the white culture, the black is an object of contempt, and therefore the target of the most vile shadow projections. In adopting the dominant cultural ideas, therefore, the black man came into conflict with his own image. He began to hate and despise himself and so cooperated in his own deprecation and subjugation. In a position analogous to Fanon's native, his situation is actually worse: he is a member of a despised minority in what is, in fact, his native land.

The current developments in race relations in the United States, the progress, if you will, can be seen as an example of what can happen as people begin to become conscious of the workings of the shadow. In addition to turning his self-hatred against the culture responsible for it, the black man in America is also attempting to raise his self-consciousness and to develop a black superego—Afro-American history, black culture, black power. Conversely, white Americans are learning to reevaluate their image of the black and so are bringing a part of their shadow to consciousness.[39] These are necessary steps if real equality between the two races is to be achieved and the material and cultural oppression of the blacks brought to an end. The

39. It is interesting to observe how the collective and conscious image of the black is improving, while on the personal and unconscious level it is often lagging behind; still, the conflict between the two images is now frequently conscious.

cultural unification and true equality of black and white Americans, however, can take place only on the superego level; for this to happen, white Americans must learn to see themselves as also black and identify with the history and cultural values of the blacks in the same way that the blacks see themselves as also white and identify with the history and the cultural values of whites. If the superegos remain separate—and unity is not just around the corner—there will be two independent cultures, which will be an improvement for the black, but will not produce true integration. And it must always be kept in mind that even cultural integration and equality are no protection against various ideological and group conflicts in which collective shadow projections may again work their destructive ways.

In the end, what is to be done with projections of the shadow? It is impossible, nor would it be desirable, to do away with them; though they may lead to catastrophic results and endanger the very survival of all involved, they are, at the same time, often necessary for psychic health. But it is possible to become cognizant of the process of projection and perhaps to temper its extreme and destructive manifestations. For this to occur, knowledge of psychological dynamics and of the contents of one's personal and collective shadow are essential. An awareness of our inadequacies and of the evil within us, the humbleness stemming from that awareness, and the strength to take an ethical stand against what we discern to be the baser drives of the psyche and of the social group are the necessary correlates. What all this really means is that in order to come to terms with shadow projections, the individual and the group must learn to be conscious of and to bear the tension of opposites within themselves. Jung thinks that on man's ability to stand this tension of opposites depends the future of mankind. For at a time when a devastating holocaust is no longer in the realm of mythology or science fiction, the withdrawal of unconscious shadow projections in politics has become a moral and biological imperative. One could say that mankind's collective shadow has grown so large and so threatening that it will no longer be possible to ignore it. It has forced on man a momentous choice—either death or psychic evolution.

6

The German Case

The developments in Germany during the first half of this century dramatically illustrate the interactions of the various historical and psychological pressures described by Jung. These forces had an effect on all of Europe; but in some countries, especially Italy, Spain, Russia, and Germany, their influence led to particularly painful results because of the peculiarity of local conditions. Given the worldwide repercussions of the German experience, and because of the Swiss cultural and geographic proximity to Germany, Jung felt impelled to subject the German case to close psychological scrutiny. Between 1936 and 1947, he wrote a number of essays dealing with the problem and had them collected and published in book form under the title *Essays on Contemporary Events.*[1]

Jung maintains that, like individuals, races, tribes, and nations "have their own peculiar psychology, and in the same way they also have their own particular kind of psychopathology."[2] The characteristic psychology of an individual, race, or

1. *Aufsätze zur Zeitgeschichte* (Zurich. 1946); English translation by E. Welsh. B. Hannah, and M. Briner, *Essays on Contemporary Events* (London: Kegan Paul. 1947).
2. "Epilogue to *Essays on Contemporary Events,"* volume 10, p. 233.

nation is formed by the interaction between inherited predispositions and environmental conditions, and these in turn are determined by and then go on to determine history, whether of the individual or the nation. In his first attempt to understand and describe the spirit stirring in Germany during the 1930s, Jung concentrates wholly upon the peculiar psychological inheritance of the Germans. This approach, he argues, explains more of what was going on in Germany than the more popular and "reasonable" economic or political elucidations.

Thus, in his 1936 essay "Wotan," he discerns a parallel between the forces active in Germany and the characteristics of Wotan (or Odin), an ancient Teutonic deity. He contends that only an immature mind considers the gods to be metaphysical entities or playful and superstitious inventions. In his view, the various gods are really personifications of basic psychic forces, primarily of the autonomous and as yet not fully conscious elements of the psyche.[3] He states that in order to avoid prejudice he could speak of the fury of the Germans and dub it the *furor teutonicus*. But such "psychologizing" of Wotan would miss the most dramatic feature of the German phenomenon—the personal experience of the "possessor" *(Ergreifer)* and the "possessed" *(Ergriffener)*. For the strangest and the most impressive thing about Germany was that "one man, who [was] obviously 'possessed,'...infected a whole nation to such an extent that everything [was] set in motion and...started rolling on its course towards perdition."[4]

As one of the chief Teutonic deities, Wotan personifies certain attributes of the Germanic psyche. He is a powerful archetype embodying the specific temperament and experience of that race, and in turn shaping its character and behavior.

3. This view is remarkably similar to that of the German materialist philosopher Ludwig Feuerbach. See his *The Essence of Christianity* (1841).
4. "Wotan," volume 10, p. 185.

Mythology describes his dominant traits. Wotan is the god of storm and frenzy, the unleasher of passions and the lust for war; he is the lord of hosts, leader of the raging warriors; he seizes men and makes them go berserk; he is a restless wanderer who creates unrest and stirs up strife wherever he goes; he is a magician and an artist of disguises; he is versed in the secrets of the occult; he is the lord of the dead warriors whom he receives into Walhalla, the hall of the slain. But he also has a more salutary side: he is the god of inspiration, poetry, and wisdom; he understands and can interpret the runes and fate. In short, he personifies the instinctual, irrational, dynamic, emotional, and inspirational aspects of the Teutonic unconscious. It does not take much insight to discern an analogy between the disturbing traits of Wotan and the psychological state of the Germans during the Nazi period: the frenzy, dynamism, wanderlust, and belligerence. An actual regression took place on the part of the masses to a more primitive German consciousness, to a time when Wotan and not the Christian God ruled.

Jung considers the Nazi development as illustration of and further evidence for the existence and power of the archetypes. Archetypes can evolve and change over time; but in the case of Wotan, first, because of the pressure of Christianity, which considered him a devil, and then because of the rationalism of the Enlightenment, which repressed him, "he simply disappeared . . . and remained invisible for more than a thousand years, working anonymously and indirectly."[5] This was the "'blond beast'. . . prowling about in its underground prison, ready at any moment to burst out with devasting consequences,"[6] about whose individual and collective reawakening Jung had warned as early as 1918. For archetypes, he writes, are like riverbeds which dry up when the water finds new channels;

5. *Ibid.*, p. 189.
6. "The Role of the Unconscious," volume 10, p. 13.

but the longer the water has flowed in the original bed, the deeper the original channel, and the more likely that sooner or later the water will return to its old course. And so, when Christianity began to lose its hold on the German society and psyche, and when situations arose that could not be dealt with in the traditionally accepted ways, the long-neglected archetype was shaken out of its "slumber" and Wotan once again began to "roam over the earth." Indeed, it probably is not pure coincidence that one of the early slogans of the Nazi movement was "Germany Awake!"

Jung thinks that many members of the German Faith Movement[7] sensed this change and openly acknowledged that the god of the Germans was no longer the Christian God but Wotan; some were even aware of their "possession" and tried to come to terms with it. Outsiders, Jung asserts, judge the Germans too much as if they were responsible agents; it would be closer to the truth to regard them as victims. He likens their lot to the Jewish experience of Yahweh, or the Arab experience of Allah, and, to an extent, commiserates with them: "It has always been terrible to fall into the hands of a living god."[8]

But because of the bipolar nature of the archetypes, Jung is hopeful that, in time, Wotan will also reveal his inspirational and mantic qualities; "if this conclusion is correct, National Socialism would not be the last word."[9] As Jung later saw, this hope was never realized.

Jung has frequently been reproached with the sin of silence and even collaboration with respect to the events in Nazi Germany. In response to these criticisms he wrote an Epilogue to

7. The German Faith Movement *(Deutsche Glaubensbewegung)*, founded in 1933 by Wilhelm Hauer, attempted to establish a German religion based on ancient Germanic and Nordic traditions and writings.
8. "Wotan," volume 10, pp. 191–92.
9. *Ibid.,* p. 192.

the *Essays on Contemporary Events* in which he compiled numerous quotations from his writings and lectures, beginning in 1918, to demonstrate his early concern with and periodic warnings against the coming threat of mass psychoses and totalitarianism in Germany and elsewhere. In addition, he explains his attitude more directly. He does not deny that at first his posture was somewhat ambivalent. He claims that initially, like so many of his contemporaries, he was disturbed by the events in Germany but could not help telling himself "that this was after all Germany, a civilized European nation with a sense of morality and discipline."[10] In a similar spirit, he was willing to grant the arguments of the many idealists of his acquaintance who maintained that the political and social abuses in Germany were regrettable, but unavoidable and temporary, and that such incidents occur at the start of any meaningful revolution. And then, on the psychological level, there was his conviction that "every archetype contains the lowest and the highest, evil and good, and is therefore capable of producing diametrically opposite results."[11] Because of this dual nature of the archetypes and the initial difficulty of predicting the direction in which they would evolve, some caution and patience were appropriate. For when an archetype is activated, its effects depend on how consciousness reacts to the situation. In therapy, Jung contends, the object is to help consciousness, through insight and understanding, to intercept and integrate the contents that are breaking through from the unconscious. The aim is to bring the positive features of the archetype into reality, while,

10. "Epilogue to *Essays on Contemporary Events*," volume 10, p. 236. See also the Appendix to volume 10 of the *Collected Works* for a discussion of the problems that arose when in 1933 Jung took over the editorship of the *Zentralblatt für Psychotherapie*, which was published in Germany.

Freud is also reported to have said at this time that "a nation that produced Goethe could not possibly go to the bad." [Ernest Jones, *The Life and Work of Sigmund Freud*, volume 3 (New York: Basic Books, 1957), p. 151.]

11. "Epilogue to *Essays on Contemporary Events*," volume 10, p. 237.

at the same time, obstructing and disarming its negative qualities. Therefore, to save what is worth saving a certain amount of optimism must be summoned even though the situation may appear depressing and hopeless. These intellectual and therapeutic considerations, Jung implies, account for his initially optimistic and later cautious attitude toward Nazi Germany.

After the war, in order to explain what had happened, Jung enlarged upon the analysis of the German psyche that he had begun in the 1936 essay on Wotan. It turned out, he observes, that Germany proved to be more vulnerable than other countries to the mass psychology that resulted from the more or less universal historical conditions that existed in Europe at the beginning of the twentieth century. He briefly alludes to some of the specifically German historical, political, social, and economic problems responsible for this increased vulnerability. For example, there was the system of moral and political education that had sought to imbue everybody with a spirit of unquestioning obedience and with a belief that every desirable thing must come from above; consequently, any feelings of personal responsibility were overshadowed by a rigid sense of duty and dependence on the state. Also, Jung thinks that the military defeat in the First World War and the social disaster that followed increased the herd instinct in Germany, making it the first victim among Western nations "of a mass movement brought about by an upheaval of forces lying dormant in the unconscious, ready to break through all moral barriers."[12] These unconscious forces were activated because of the accumulation of faulty conscious attitudes and troublesome external conditions. To the then generally prevailing sense of confusion and impotence in Europe were added the military defeat, political humiliation, social disorientation, economic depression, cul-

12. "The Fight with the Shadow," volume 10, p. 219.

tural nihilism, and the overall instability and chaos of the Weimar period in Germany. Under such a concentrated barrage it is not surprising that Germany succumbed to a compensating form of mass psychosis: the traditionally sanctioned conscious attitudes could no longer effectively aid the individual to cope with the threatening and insecure environment.

The unconscious elements mobilized were those that would compensate for the conditions that produced the crisis in consciousness. And since, in spite of the many qualities that Germans share with all mankind, they "undoubtedly have their own peculiar psychology which distinguishes them from their neighbors,"[13] the compensatory forces embodied and were expressed through these specifically national traits. Thus, to the Wotan archetype, which explains certain characteristics of the Nazi movement, Jung now adds the German feeling of inferiority and analyzes the developments in Germany from this vantage point. He does not delve fully into the historical and temperamental reasons for these feelings. He merely asserts their existence and then emphasizes that their exacerbation during the postwar era led to the need for a radical compensation.

Generally speaking, feelings of inferiority, irrespective of their origin, tend to "make people touchy and lead to compensatory efforts to impress."[14] Consequently, "the German thrusts himself forward and seeks to curry favour, or 'German efficiency' is demonstrated with...aplomb" even in cases of organized murder.[15] That murder is being committed in the process is secondary to the considerations of efficiency and prestige. Similarly, the Nazi preoccupation with power, authority, and superiority, the pretensions of the *Herrenmensch* and

13. "After the Catastrophe," volume 10, p. 210.
14. *Ibid.*, p. 202
15. *Ibid.*

the *Herrenvolk* were all motivated by deep-seated and aggravated feelings of inferiority.

Inferiority feelings are not always unjustified; frequently they are "a sign of inferior feeling—which is not just a play on words."[16] This is particularly true in the case of the Germans, in Jung's opinion. Seen in this light, their "obsession"—for that is often the most accurate description—with intellectual sophistication and technological precision serves, on the one hand, to compensate for an inferior and undifferentiated feeling function, and, on the other hand, to divert energy and attention away from a painful inferiority. From this perspective, Nazi anti-Semitism takes on another aspect in addition to the need for a scapegoat during times of crisis. For one could argue that the Jewish culture, to a greater degree than the German, has developed the feeling side of the psyche; and the confrontation with one's "inferior" function, whether in oneself or others, always poses a threat. Hence the need to compensate, to repress the "inferiority," to dispose of the threat.

When speaking of the "inferior" feelings of an individual or a group, Jung does not mean to imply that the individual or the group is in fact inferior; he merely points to the fact that there is a place of weakness—"a peculiar instability, which exists independently of all the other qualities."[17] The inferiority is rarely conscious; mostly it is only dimly suspected, although the unconscious is "aware" of it and motivates the various attempts at compensation. The division between the "superior" and the "inferior" functions in the psyche can lead to a hysterical dissociation of the personality, to a separation of the opposites which are normally held together. Opposites are inherent in every psyche: men have a feminine side, women a masculine; the

16. *Ibid.*
17. *Ibid.*, p. 207.

intelligent have their stupid side, the courageous their cowardly side, and so on. In a hysterical personality, those opposites that particularly affect character become separated more than in most people. The greater "distance" then produces a higher tension with a resulting increase in energy and drive. A good part of the dynamism of the Germans during the Nazi period was undoubtedly connected with the development of an ever increasing "distance" between the intellect and feeling, between the conscious refinement of thought and the repressed undifferentiated emotions. Moreover, ignorance of one's "other" side, together with an inkling of its primitive force, intensifies any already present feelings of inadequacy and fear. This is a new feeling of inferiority added to the original one, and the compounded sense of inferiority and insecurity is "the source of the hysteric's prestige psychology, of his need to make an impression, to flaunt his merits and insist on them;...it is the cause of that loud-mouthed arrogance, uppishness, insolence, and tactlessness by which so many Germans, who at home grovel like dogs, win a bad reputation for their countrymen abroad."[18]

The hysterical disposition is therefore partially based on and invariably accompanied by ignorance and repression of the shadow, of every weak and displeasing trait of the personality. The hysteric is aware only of his good motives and praiseworthy characteristics. When the baser motives or traits become evident, he lies and then believes his own lies, or he "becomes the unscrupulous Superman and *Herrenmensch* who fancies he is ennobled by the magnitude of his aim."[19] The repression of the shadow and the lack of awareness of it also mean that it is projected onto others, and that everything evil, inferior, and culpable is found outside oneself. Hence the claim that one is

18. *Ibid.*, p. 208.
19. *Ibid.*, pp. 207–8.

surrounded by people, or one's country is surrounded by countries, who are inappreciative, inferior, or activated only by hostile motives, and the consequent need to subdue, denigrate, torment, or even terrorize them. Since both internally and externally there is a loss of a sense of perspective and proportion, the compensation in this case is achieved by poses and boasts of "ice-cold" realism.

Given the German tendency, as Jung sees it, toward this kind of psychological imbalance, together with the confused and chaotic conditions of the Weimar period, there arose in Germany a countervailing need for stability and order. On the basis of his experience with patients afflicted by similar, although individual, conditions and symptoms, Jung states that if such an "individual was able to cling to a shred of reason, or to preserve the bonds of a human relationship, a new compensation was brought about in the unconscious by the very chaos of the conscious mind."[20] New symbols arose in dreams or during "active imagination" representing the forces of order; invariably these symbols, of a measured and symmetrical nature, resembled the axial system known as the mandala.[21] When unconscious, these symbols are predominantly of a collective nature; however, they can be brought to consciousness and integrated with the individual personality. On the other hand, if the forces they represent are left to accumulate in the unconscious to a dangerous degree, they then encroach upon consciousness and take it by surprise and violence. "Organized" mass movements,

20. "The Fight with the Shadow," volume 10, p. 220.
21. *Active imagination* is Jung's term for the conscious observation of and reaction to the images and symbols of the unconscious; the process could be described as "conscious dreaming," although it is not spontaneous, but directed. In many ways, it is identical to certain forms of meditation. For a detailed exposition of the mandala, see *Psychology and Alchemy*, volume 12 of the *Collected Works*. See also "A Study in the Process of Individuation" and "Concerning Mandala Symbolism" in volume 9, part 1. And for an excellent outline of the Indian conception of the mandala, see Giuseppe Tucci, *The Theory and Practice of the Mandala* (London. Rider & Co., 1969).

and the "unity" achieved through collectivism or totalitarianism
are the results. These movements in turn mobilize other collective elements of the unconscious and so compound the problem.
And that, Jung suggests, is what happened in Germany. Finally,
where the society is in disarray, where individuals are atomized
and then brought together in mass organizations, and where the
unconscious forces of order are mobilized, there arises the need
for a leader. And here, too, the collective archetypal heritage
plays a role, for the leader imago, the powerful, effective,
magical personality, is one of the primal archetypes of mankind.
Under the proper conditions, any likely figure can become the
object for the projection of this archetype.

For a number of reasons, then, the Germans were prone to
mass psychology and collective psychic inflation. Moreover, both
of these phenomena went largely unopposed, for there are few
better forms of compensation for feelings of inferiority,
weakness, isolation, and insecurity than mass groupings and
psychic inflation. Even prior to the Weimar experience, the German psyche had expressed, in Jung's view, a longing to transcend the limitations of human nature. Goethe's Faust and Nietzsche's Zarathustra are the literary representations of this
psychological drive. Once "god was dead," it was only a matter
of time before this yearning, which formerly found an outlet in
religion and mysticism, took on a more materialistic form. Jung
writes that the Germans could have learned something from
Nietzsche's disastrous personal attempt to reach the realm
"beyond good and evil." But the lesson went unnoticed, and instead the attempt was made in the field of politics. The consequences were what might have been expected from such a
"beyond-human" identification with and misappropriation of
power. For the sense of "'God-Almightiness' does not make
man divine, it merely fills him with arrogance and arouses

everything evil in him. It produces a diabolical caricature of man, and this inhuman mask is so unendurable, such a torture to wear, that he tortures others."[22]

Jung acknowledges that it is not without misgivings that he pins the labels of "psychopathic inferiority" and "hysteria" onto an entire nation.[23] But in his opinion, national psychology is merely a more complex form of individual psychology and therefore liable to the same disturbances, and only the psychological condition of the Germans at the time, Jung insists, can explain how they could have followed a man who was clearly mentally deranged. Otherwise, it is impossible "to understand how his ranting speeches, delivered in shrill, grating, womanish tones, could have made such an impression."[24] His theatrical and clearly hysterical gestures struck all foreigners as ridiculous. "He behaved in public like a man living in his own biography, in this case as the sombre, daemonic 'man of iron' of popular fiction. . . . He was an utterly incapable, unadapted, irresponsible, psychopathic personality full of empty, infantile fantasies, but cursed with the keen intuition of a rat or a guttersnipe."[25] Yet to the Germans, he was normal and impressive, for he expressed their actual condition: their frustration, their anger, their collective hysteria. He personally embodied all the traits typical of the hysteric: "complete lack of insight into one's own character, auto-erotic self-admiration and self-extenuation, denigration and terrorization of one's fellow men (how contemptuously Hitler spoke of his own people!), projection of the shadow, lying,

22. "After the Catastrophe," volume 10, p. 215.
23. Jung thinks that saying the Germans were psychologically ill is kinder than saying that they were criminals: "a medical diagnosis is not an accusation, an illness is not a disgrace but a misfortune" ("Epilogue to *Essays on Contemporary Events,*" volume 10, p. 241). Still, even though there may exist good reasons for either crime or insanity, it does not follow that their consequences are to be ignored or completely excused.
24. "After the Catastrophe," volume 10, p. 204.
25. *Ibid.,* and "The Fight with the Shadow," volume 10, p. 223.

falsification of reality, determination to impress by fair means or foul, bluffing and double-crossing."[26] A clinical diagnosis of Hitler's condition would be *pseudologia phantastica:* the form of hysteria characterized by a talent for believing one's own lies.

In addition to hysteria, Hitler also represented, in Jung's opinion, the shadow side, the repressed "inferior" side, of the German personality. His character and his life were made up of painful inadequacies, childish emotions, and an all-consuming drive for power and superiority. This part of his personality also heightened his popularity, for under certain conditions a sense of recognition and a feeling of exhilaration may accompany a meeting with the formerly repressed shadow; there is always a fascination, even empathy, connected with the observation of the antics of the collective trickster figure. But while he expressed the German hysterical, inferior, and shadow sides, Hitler also represented and promised the various psychological and social compensations that the Germans required—power, authority, superiority, respect, security, discipline, and order. That for almost ten years he succeeded in providing these, even if, at times, only in appearance, also helps to account for his hold over the German people. Nor is the Nazi ideological and ritual appeal to the unconscious tribal memory of the Teutonic race to be lightly dismissed. "Wotan" had his grip on the Germans, and Hitler and the Nazis made deliberate use of powerful unconscious forces, while at the same time serving as their instruments.

Such, in Jung's view, was the general psychological syndrome responsible for the Germany catastrophe. After the debacle, the question of "collective guilt" arose. Although legally, and even morally, collective guilt may be a tenuous concept, psychologically—as the irrational presence of a subjective

26. "After the Catastrophe," volume 10, p. 203.

feeling of guilt—it is, in Jung's opinion, a fact. "Psychological collective guilt is a *tragic fate*. It hits everybody, just and unjust alike, everybody who was anywhere near the place where the terrible thing happened," or even remotely associated with it.[27] On the archaic and primitive level, it brings about a state of "magical uncleanness" which necessitates some form of purification. Thus, there is no doubt that in the eyes of the rest of the world, the European, and in the eyes of Europeans, the German is a guilty man. From the psychological point of view, Jung notes, it hardly matters whether the man responsible for a particular crime is named Müller or Meier. The fact is that the German has betrayed the noblest values of the Judeo-Christian civilization, and "has fallen on his European brethren like a beast of prey, and tortured and murdered them."[28] The disappointment is all the more bitter because, given recognized German achievements, the expectations were so very different.

But psychological collective guilt for the Nazi catastrophe is not restricted to Germany. For psychologically, the fact is that "the sight of evil kindles evil in the soul."[29] The mere witnessing of a crime has a pernicious effect upon the psyche. "We are all so much a part of the human community that every crime calls forth a secret satisfaction in some corner of the fickle human heart."[30] In more suggestion-prone psyches the sight of a crime may enhance the susceptibility to infection and imitation: hence the series of similar crimes that often follows the featuring of a particular offense by the news media. But every psyche is fascinated by evil. "One should not imagine for a moment that

27. *Ibid.*, p. 197. "Collective guilt" is something about which every immigrant to the United States quickly learns. Even though he has no personal relation to the enslavement and segregation of blacks, his mere presence in the country soon makes him feel responsible and guilty as well.

28. *Ibid.*

29. *Ibid.*, p. 199.

30. *Ibid.*, p. 198.

anybody could escape this play of opposites. Even a saint would have to pray unceasingly for the souls of Hitler and Himmler, the Gestapo and the S.S., in order to repair without delay the damage done to his own soul.''[31] In most men the evil so kindled is disguised as moral indignation, and this does have its beneficial effects. For evil demands expiation; otherwise the wicked would destroy the world, or the good suffocate in their own rage. The only danger is that the moral outrage inspired by baleful acts, but fueled by the vice present in every psyche, may surpass in iniquity the original mischief.

At any rate, in order to ensure that a similar catastrophe does not recur, Jung argues that Germans should become aware of their psychological makeup and learn to deal consciously with their feelings of inferiority and the shadow side of their psyche. To atone for their moral failure and reduce the effects of their psychological anxiety they should willingly acknowledge their collective guilt. Attempts to minimize, excuse, or rationalize what occurred merely conceal an amalgam of guilt, repentance, and a desire for revenge. Such attitudes are of little value morally, and psychologically they still represent attempts to compensate for a sense of inferiority and failure, and a refusal to recognize the shadow. The psychological state that contributed so greatly to the Nazi phenomenon in the first place is thereby perpetuated.

But all this, Jung intimates, is perhaps asking too much of the Germans, because neither their psychological instability nor their collective guilt is fully their own responsibility. The German catastrophe was really only one crisis in a general European illness, and what happened in Germany was the outcome of psychic conditions that are more or less universal. Therefore conscious participation in the collective guilt of the Germans is

31. *Ibid.*, p. 199.

called for on the part of all mankind, as is the necessity for psychological self-knowledge, if similar catastrophes are to be avoided elsewhere. In the absence of a sense of responsibility for the political tragedies of our day and with ignorance of the psychological processes that help bring them about, all attempts to achieve peace and harmony consist of empty words at best, and if forced on people are dangerous to their well-being. But although conscientious empathy and psychological understanding would be a great step forward, alone they will not suffice; no neurotic, Jung maintains, was ever cured by mere "understanding" of his problems. No amount of understanding will solve the problem of the shadow or do away with the existence of evil. Jung insists that a complete spiritual renewal is needed if these problems are to be meaningfully dealt with. But such a spiritual rebirth cannot be achieved through collective measures or through old religious formulas. Only individual efforts to attain self-knowledge and development can give birth to a new attitude that will then alter the political and social aspects of mankind's existence.

Almost every psychological study of the Nazi period concentrates on the mental attributes of the German people. Jung's analysis is no exception. The personality of Hitler is not regarded as the primary factor; rather it is seen as a complementary aspect of a general German syndrome. Yet, considering the impact of Hitler on European history and his clearly pathological behavior, it is odd that there have appeared so few serious psychological studies of his personality. Jung offers a sketchy, impressionistic diagnosis—hysteria and pathological inferiority—while at the same time indicating that the problem goes beyond mere medical categories. The most extensive analysis to date is a recently published 1943 report written for the Office of Strategic Services, entitled *The Mind of Adolf Hitler* by Walter C. Langer.[32] The study indicates that the personality of Hitler was unusually complex to start with and was made more so by the situation in which he found himself and which he helped to create.

His initial psychological condition seems to have been characterized by intense oedipal conflict, repercussions from the early death of his parents, a fixation on adolescent rebellion, poor social adaptation, an ambivalent attitude toward women, similar ambivalence toward authority and domination, passive feminine qualities, latent homosexuality, apparent monorchism, feelings of inferiority, masochism, coprophagic tendencies, the fear of death, hypochondria, and an inclination toward hysteria. Faced with such a barrage of problems, conflicts, fears, and inferiorities, it is remarkable that Hitler, after years of illness, floundering, and despondency (from 1905 through 1914) was able to marshall enough strength and imagination to make an attempt to overcome them. The psychological problems he had to deal with were enormous and far from the usual lot that most people must resolve in order to chart a course in life and find some satisfaction for themselves. It is little wonder, therefore, that the search for a solution led Hitler along strange paths and required uncommon efforts and compensations, which included such peculiarities as vegetarianism, anti-Semitism, paranoia, mysticism, messiah and superman complexes, psychic inflation, an excessive will to power, an emphasis on virility, action, and aggression, and an identification with passion, instinct, and the power of the unconscious. Obviously his compensations brought him to the brink of madness and had they remained on a per-

32. Walter C. Langer, *The Mind of Adolf Hitler* (New York: Signet, 1973). Erik Erikson, who apparently was acquainted with the Langer report and used some of its theses, has an excellent essay on "The Legend of Hitler's Childhood" in his book, *Childhood and Society*, rev. ed. (New York: Norton, 1964).

sonal level that would probably have been the result.

However, in cases of severe psychological malaise, it often happens that the individual is unable to contain the pressures and is forced to externalize and universalize his personal problems. He finds relief by projecting his undesirable traits onto others; he reverses the flow of energy from inner repression and guilt to outer conflict and censure, thereby freeing his psyche for other functions. As a result, sometimes he is able to gain a broader perspective on the nature of his difficulties and turn his weaknesses into strengths. For those with the appropriate talents, art and literature are the usual realms for this "sublimation" of personal problems into larger human and aesthetically interesting themes. For more ordinary mortals, religion at one time served this purpose. But today, the most popular sphere for such externalization is politics.

Harold D. Lasswell, who pioneered the use of psychoanalytic concepts in political science, has devised a formula to describe the process. The political type, Lasswell observes, is a person who displaces his private drives onto the public realm and rationalizes them in terms of the public good. Since power is the aim of politics, Lasswell assumes that an individual undertakes such a displacement—consciously or unconsciously—to satisfy an ungratified craving for deference; as a means of compensation for material, physical, or psychological deprivation; or to overcome low estimates of the self or of the group with which he identifies.

Clearly, Hitler is an outstanding example of the political type. He managed to identify his personal problems and inferiorities with the weak, humiliated, disturbed, and unstable Germany of the Weimar period, and to convince himself that his own peculiar compensations were also the qualities necessary for Germany if it was to overcome its difficulties and achieve future stability and growth. Such displacement and identification made Hitler a political man, but they would not, of themselves, have sufficed to make him a successful political leader. For this, he had to acquire the necessary skills of a politician. Given the nature of his complexes, he obviously could not enter politics as a member of parliament. The form of his political involvement had to be in accord with his character. His eventual success was due in no small measure to his ability to learn and make use of political skills that suited his temperament, while concurrently persuading a good part of the German public that his manner of seeing and doing politics was appropriate and effective. In this context, his flair for oratory; the histrionic ability through which he exploited his hysteria in calculated rages; his effective use of mass psychology, propaganda, images, and symbols; his cultivation of charisma; his capacity for action and for inspiring the action and devotion of others; and his political intuition are the aspects of his personality that come to the fore. His development as a political leader was complete when he linked his now personal-national compensations, concerns, and methods of action with a compatible ideology, the Fascist doctrine, with its emphasis on virility, power, racism, and millenarianism. And since his adoption of Fascism was initially motivated by the intensity of his personal needs and drives, it followed that he embodied the doctrine personally, as *Herrenmensch,* messiah, god. He succeeded, at least for a time, in turning his private psychotic compensatory illusions into reality.

Langer, in concluding his analysis of Hitler, makes the following apposite observations:

It is Hitler's ability to play upon the unconscious tendencies of the German people and to act as their spokesman that has enabled him to mobilize their energies and direct them into the same channels through which he believed he had found a solution to his own personal conflicts. The result has been an extraordinary similarity in thinking, feeling, and acting in the German people. It is as though Hitler had paralyzed the critical functions of the individual Germans and had assumed the role for himself. As such he has been incorporated as a part of the personalities of his individual supporters and is able to dominate their mental processes. ... In fighting for Hitler these persons are now unconsciously fighting for what appears to them to be their own psychological integrity.[33]

The fact that a psychopath became the ego ideal and the symbol of the Self for an entire people was a clear indication of their collectively disturbed psychological state. The case is disconcerting for those contemporary historians and social scientists who would like to dismiss the influence of personality on history. It illustrates that one individual, in the course of working out his own personal problems, can disrupt the peace of the world and lead a good part of mankind to perdition and madness.

Taking into account the conditions of the time and the effects of the man, one is tempted to conclude that had the personality been somewhat different, the results might not have been the same. The Weimar period was ripe for the appearance of a charismatic leader and a salvationist myth or millenarian movement. That it was Hitler, with all his peculiarities, who stepped in at that precise moment was surely historical accident. Similar conditions at other times and in other countries have been met by leaders whose personality allowed for the development of some of the more positive aspects of the unconscious forces mobilized. For the salvationist myth, once activated, can move men either toward the creation of a new community and a new psychic integration, or toward frenzied madness and Armageddon.

Jung's investigation of the unconscious and its frequently per-

33. Langer, *The Mind of Adolf Hitler*, p. 209.

nicious influence on group psychology made him wary of mass movements and mass psychology. Nonetheless, with all its primitive and destructive tendencies, the unconscious is also the mainspring of man's creativity and evolution; it contains almost equal potential for good and evil. Mass movements and the manifestations of mass psychology, therefore, are not always to be rejected out of hand or subjugated to rational control; often, they are the bearers of new and useful forces that have a momentous effect on the historical and psychological development of mankind.

It was this guardedly favorable notion of the unconscious and of the collective movements that reflect and express its drives that was responsible, in part, for Jung's wait-and-see attitude at the outset of the Nazi movement. He recognized that external events had brought many Germans under the sway of powerful unconscious drives and concluded that it would be best not to attack the already beleaguered and unstable national ego. He hoped that as the aroused energies played themselves out, the more creative elements of the German character would come to the surface with equal dynamism. For these reasons, Jung decided to retain a medical perspective on events and to reserve his moral and political judgment. He did this in spite of his own previous warnings of the dangers associated with mass psychic epidemics, and the collectivism and totalitarianism that inevitably follow them. Thus, like many statesmen of the time, and for somewhat the same reasons, Jung at first advocated appeasement. Both the statesmen and Jung took a calculated risk and lived to regret their decision: they misjudged the intensity of the problem and the personality of Hitler.

For a confirmed liberal, or for members of the races that were the target of Nazi venom, Jung's initial ambivalence, his vacillation, even if motivated by the best intentions, is reprehensible. From a more general point of view it can be excused as the result of mistaken expectations and political naiveté. But his placing of the topic of differences in racial psychology on the program of the International Society for Psychotherapy during his tenure as its president (1933–1939) was a stupid and callous act for which there is really no excuse. This is not the place to go into the details of his professional activities at the time, but these included, in addition to the above, his working with a Nazified German Section of the International Society for Psychotherapy and his management of the *Zentralblatt für Psychotherapie* on which M. H. Göring, a psychiatrist and a cousin of Reichsmarschall Göring, served as co-editor. Thus, there may be some basis for allegations that, at least to begin with, Jung was not unsympathetic to National Socialism.

But there were also more salutary actions on Jung's part with respect to the Nazis, especially with regard to the Jewish question. During his presidency, the International Society for Psychotherapy took in German-Jewish doctors who were excluded from the "Nazified" German Section. Because of his insistence, the Society remained "neutral as to politics and creed," and the *Zentralblatt* continued to publish unbiased reviews of books by Jewish authors. In 1934, Jung included in his book *Wirklichkeit der Seele* a contribution by a Jewish author, Hugo Rosenthal, and in the same year, wrote a foreword to *Entdeckung der Seele*, a book by his Jewish pupil Gerhard Adler. Thus there is little if any evidence to show that Jung himself was anti-Semitic. By 1936, in his essay on "Wotan," he had come to essentially negative conclusions about the "possession" of the Germans. And he resigned his presidency of the International Society in 1939, when it was overwhelmed by large Italian, Hungarian, and even Japanese groups, and he could no longer get assurances that it would remain free of "Aryan" regulations.[34]

Thus, although he made some serious errors, Jung was far from being a Nazi or an anti-Semite. Furthermore, the contributions he has made to human knowledge and the capacity of his personality and ideas to inspire the best in others must compensate, in some measure at least, for his mistakes and are not affected by them. If anything, the disclosure of his politically unadapted shadow side will check any tendencies on the part of his admirers to turn him into something more than a man who happened to be endowed with a number of unusual talents.

34. The most balanced and complete treatment of the entire issue of Jung's relationship with National Socialism appears to be an essay by Aniela Jaffé, "C. G. Jung and National Socialism," in her book, *From the Life and Work of C. G. Jung*, trans. by Richard F. Hull (New York: Harper & Row, 1970). A perusal of Jung's letters during this period tends to clarify his motives and conveys a more favorable impression of his activities and attitudes than the mere "facts" would seem to warrant. See *The C. G. Jung Letters: 1906–1950*, volume 1, eds. Gerhard Adler and Aniela Jaffé, Bollingen Series 95 (Princeton: Princeton University Press, 1973).

7

The End of Politics

In these times it is impossible to discuss the future of man without keeping in mind the ever-present threat of an atomic war that could well annihilate all human life. Unfortunately, this statement has by now deteriorated into a ritual intonation at the beginning of all political tracts, so that its meaning no longer penetrates into consciousness. Moreover, people prefer to deal with this threat as they do with their personal death: they tend to ignore it or leave it up to fate. Such attitudes may be valid and even beneficial with respect to individual life, but they are inappropriate and dangerous to the life of the species. From that perspective, it is criminal and the height of human stupidity and immorality for any individual or group to ignore or accept fatalistically the possibility of a worldwide nuclear conflagration that would make the last world war seem like child's play.

In addition to the historical, military, and political forces that make the possibility of nuclear war ever-present, there are psychological forces that cannot be dismissed lightly. These derive from the power and primitivity of the human instincts, the general human ignorance of the unconscious, and the consequent frailty of conscious responsibility and morality. "The situation is about the same as if a small boy of six had been given a bag of dynamite for a birthday present. We are not one hundred percent convinced by his assurances that no calamity will happen."[1] Because of the danger, Jung, in an unusually militant mood, even proposes that "any government of impassioned patriots which signs the order for mobilization should immediately be executed *en bloc*."[2] But at the same time, he repeatedly argues that all attempts to outlaw war or armaments permanently are naive and unrealistic. As far as he is concerned, it would be comparable to outlawing sexual intercourse. He is convinced that "man's war-like instincts are ineradicable," and that *"homo homini lupus* is a sad yet eternal truism."[3] The instincts for power and aggression are as fundamental to man as the instincts for sex and affection; for as paradoxical as it may seem today, the power instincts also contribute to the self-preservation of the species and to the psychic health of the individual. Instincts can be modified, sublimated, and balanced, but they cannot be eliminated, and certainly not by decree.

Democracy, Jung thinks, is one way of modifying and balancing the warlike instincts politically: it allows them to "expend themselves in the form of domestic quarrels called 'political life.' "[4] He argues that democracy is really a "highly psychological institution which takes account of human nature as it is and makes allowances for the necessity of conflict within its own national boundaries."[5] In a democracy, the individual's frequent enmity toward others, his need for aggressiveness, and his

1. "Epilogue to *Essays on Contemporary Events,*" volume 10, p. 242.
2. *Ibid.,* p. 243.
3. "The Fight with the Shadow," volume 10, p. 225, and "Epilogue to *Essays on Contemporary Events,*" volume 10, p. 231.
4. "The Fight with the Shadow," volume 10, p. 224.
5. *Ibid.,* p. 225.

desire for power are given free reign within the limits of a constitution, law, and a tolerable level of crime and corruption. It is not too far off the mark to say that democracy is a chronic state of mitigated civil war and anarchy. But by accepting, introverting, and then limiting the instincts for hostility and aggression to the domestic sphere, democracy, to a certain extent, decreases the need for foreign enemies and wars. Jung maintains that both domestic and foreign conflicts could be reduced still further if men learned *consciously* to introvert some of their aggressiveness directly into their own psyches. Much of the "national, mitigated state of war would soon come to an end if everybody could see his own shadow and begin the only struggle that is really worth while: the fight against the overwhelming power-drive of the shadow."[6]

This analysis and prescription should not be taken to mean that all political conflicts are ultimately a product of psychological drives. But it does mean that, as long as these drives remain unconscious, they often provoke and always participate in conflicts that on the surface appear to be purely political; for the *unconscious* repression of aggression leads to a personal sense of anxiety and guilt and then frequently to external hostility and aggression. Thus, in many instances, political antagonisms and conflicts are a masked and projected expression of internal psychological struggles. Jung believes that an understanding of the contents and the behavior of the unconscious, particularly of the inferior elements that seek compensation through aggression and power, would drastically reduce political conflict and place it in a more realistic perspective. Psychological self-knowledge and the mutual withdrawal of hostile projections are among the prerequisites for a more peaceful domestic and international order.

6. *Ibid.*, p. 224.

Jung does not believe that a state of perfect peace, whether individual or social, is possible or even desirable; for in any more
or less permanently balanced condition "one is threatened with
suffocation and unbearable ennui," so that a perfect balance
seeks an imbalance and perfect peace breeds war.[7] However, a
modicum of peace is both possible and desirable, and today, absolutely necessary. But even limited peace will not be achieved
without a struggle, for the natural condition of man is to be in a
state of war—with his physical and social environment and with
his own rebellious instinctual nature. Hence, the establishment
of even a limited peace—moods and actions that are serene,
deliberate, and well-balanced—requires the painstaking
development of new and conscious attitudes and certainly cannot be effected without the cooperation of the individual.

By now it should be abundantly clear that for Jung the
psychology of a nation reflects the psychology of its individuals,
and only appropriate psychological changes in its individual
citizens can initiate a change in the psychology of a nation.
Abolition of the old order and establishment of worldwide
brotherhood and peace cannot be accomplished by propaganda,
social engineering, and agitation, or by political, economic, or
humanitarian revolutions. The revolutions must first take place
within the individual, and it is meaningless to speak of national
or international peace until individuals achieve a degree of conscious harmony among the warring powers of their own psyches.
"The great problems of humanity," Jung contends, "were never
yet solved by general laws, but only through regeneration of the
attitudes of individuals."[8] Unfortunately, few men recognize this
or undertake the difficult personal psychological task involved,
and those who do are usually not the political leaders of

7. "Analytical Psychology and 'Weltanschauung,' " volume 8, p. 360.
8. *Two Essays*, volume 7, p. 4.

mankind. When social problems arise, people tend to assume that their solution must also be social, and they find it easier to deal with them through political and institutional reforms, or by demanding changes on the part of others. Consequently, they force improvements upon their "neighbours under the hypocritical cloak of Christian love or the sense of social responsibility or any of the other beautiful euphemisms for unconscious urges to personal power."[9] Needless to say, nothing fundamental is altered by such methods, and the same problems reappear, although perhaps in other guises.

One of the positive results of the many shocking political experiences of this century is that people have become skeptical of political ideologies and of all grandiose plans for world reform. The once staunch faith in reason, science, progress, material welfare, and humanitarianism has been eroded. The various modern dreams of a millenium to be achieved through the rational organization of the world have faded: "Neither the Christian Church, nor the brotherhood of man, nor international social democracy, nor the solidarity of economic interests has stood up to the acid test of reality."[10] The danger of nuclear annihilation, the revelation by psychology of man's basic irrationality, and the unconscious, often unsavory, nature of his strivings have all compounded man's doubts about himself and about his future.

In an extraordinarily prescient essay, "The Spiritual Problem of Modern Man," written in 1928, Jung describes some of these problems and attempts a prognosis. He distinguishes the "modern man" from the man who merely happens to be alive at the present time. He asserts that from a psychological point of view, the lowest level of every civilized community lives in "a

9. *Ibid.,* p. 5.
10. "The Spiritual Problem of Modern Man," volume 10, p. 77.

state of unconsciousness little different from that of primitives. Those of the ... [middle] strata live on a level of consciousness which corresponds to the beginnings of human culture, while those of the highest stratum [modern men] have a consciousness that reflects the life of the last few centuries."[11] This is a psychological, not a socioeconomic classification, and there is no necessary correlation with educational background. Nor does it mean that the people on the lower levels are not all affected by the forces operative at the time in which they live; in fact, the lower the level of consciousness, the stronger and more direct the impact of the times upon the unconscious. Thus, men on the lowest levels of consciousness frequently reflect the temper of their time in their attitudes and behavior more faithfully than those on the higher levels where other influences are at work, but they are not aware of the reasons for their reactions. The "modern man" alone has a consciousness that exists in the immediate present. He is fully aware of the factors determining his attitudes and behavior, and therefore he alone deals with the actual problems of the day. The values and the strivings of the past no longer interest him except from the historical standpoint. "He has become 'unhistorical' in the deepest sense and has estranged himself from the mass of men who live entirely within the bounds of tradition."[12] But to be unhistorical, to attain a higher level of consciousness, is to commit the Promethean sin, and so, together with his emancipation, the modern man experiences a sense of guilt. Moreover, because he lives on the edge of history and stands before "the Nothing out of which All may grow," he is cognizant of his responsibility for choosing his past and his future, and he feels the angst that accompanies

11. *Ibid.*, p. 75.
12. *Ibid.*

knowledge of the fact that everything is possible.[13]

Since there is always "snob appeal" and a feeling of exhilaration attached to the flouting of tradition and the declaration of freedom, it is usual for many people to give themselves airs of modernity. To affect a consciousness of the present is not difficult and even entails a degree of anguish, guilt, and loneliness, although in this case these feelings are based on "bad faith," to paraphrase Sartre. At any rate, such pseudomoderns suddenly "appear by the side of the truly modern man—uprooted wraiths, blood-sucking ghosts whose emptiness casts discredit upon him in his unenviable loneliness."[14] And because they call themselves modern, and through their antics, ostentatious rebellion, and wailing come to the attention of the public, the really modern man is often found among those who call themselves old-fashioned. In this way, he dissociates himself from the pseudomoderns and makes some amends for his break with tradition. To deny the past only for the sake of being conscious of the present is meaningless and characteristic of the pseudomoderns. For the truly modern man, the present has meaning not as a denial of the past, but as a creative transition point between the past and the future. Creativity based on proficiency is an excellent criterion by which to distinguish the modern man from his pseudomodern counterpart: "The idea of proficiency is especially repugnant to the pseudomoderns, for it reminds them of their trickery,"[15] which is especially obvious in their solipsistic and bizarre attempts to be creative and original. The modern man, on the other hand, is proficient in the best sense: he has accomplished as much as the other people of his culture, and even a little more (obviously, the measure here is not

13. *Ibid.* In addition to the generally known myth that he stole fire from the gods and gave it to man, Prometheus is also a trickster figure and preserver of men; his name means "Fore-thinker."

14. *Ibid.,* p. 76.

15. *Ibid.*

material success or popular acclaim), and in this way has atoned for and partially justified his break with the past.

Whatever elation or exhilaration the modern man may have felt as a result of his clear awareness of the present and his freedom from the past is soon revealed to him to be unjustified: he merely needs to reflect briefly upon the fact that nearly two thousand years of Christian idealism have not been followed by the return of the Messiah and the establishment of the Kingdom of God, but by the rise of tyrants, atheistic totalitarian states, and organized mass murder. The post-Christian spirit turns out to be composed of "a false spirit of arrogance, hysteria, wooly-mindedness, criminal amorality, and doctrinaire fanaticism, a purveyor of shoddy spiritual goods, spurious art, philo-sophical stutterings, and Utopian humbug, fit only to be fed wholesale to the mass man of today."[16] Who can feel pride or joy in such a historical outcome? The evidence demands hum-bleness. Modern man may be the culmination of a historical era, but he is at the same time a woeful disappointment to the hopes of mankind. Recognizing these facts, questioning all past and present ideals, and being sceptical of the latest palliative measures, modern man suffers from severe psychological shock and as a result lives in a state of profound uncertainty and distress.

After four centuries during which Western man's psychic energies were directed with trust and optimism outward toward the objective world, this outward flow is today encountering ob-structions. For many people, what goes on in the objective world has become too ugly to look at and too hopeless to reflect upon. For them, "the day's life is such a bad dream that they long for the night when the spirit awakes."[17] Because of his disillusion-

16. *Aion: Researches into the Phenomenology of the Self,* volume 9, part 2, p. 35.
17. "The Spiritual Problem of Modern Man," volume 10, p. 93.

ment and scepticism modern man is thrown back on himself. "His energies flow towards their source, and the collision washes to the surface those psychic contents which are at all times there, but lie hidden in the silt so long as the stream flows smoothly in its course."[18] The result of this turning inward has been the birth of the modern science of psychology. The psyche was always present, but previously, aside from the more bizarre objective manifestations of disturbances within, there was little interest in it. In the twentieth century it could no longer be ignored, and Western man turned to it as his last refuge, only to discover that like the external world, the psyche, too, is full of chaos, strife, ugliness, and evil; after four centuries of neglect and repression, Jung adds, this is hardly surprising. For many people it actually comes as a relief to find so much evil in the depths of the psyche: here at last, they feel, is the root of all the evil in the world. With the same optimism that was previously directed to the objective world, such people now believe that all of man's problems can be solved through analysis, therapy, and psychologically oriented education. But even though the conclusion is facile, the acceptance of the importance of turning inward is a step in the right direction.

Contemporary man's fascination with the psyche is so strong that he does not shirk even when he finds it to be full of contents that disgust and repel him. The interest is not merely morbid or perverse; rather, modern man expects something from the psyche that the outer world has failed to give him, something that religion provided in the past but no longer provides—at least for modern man—namely, inner experience and inner revelation. This is why the fascination with the psyche is not limited to fascination with psychology as a science, or with Freudian psychoanalysis, but includes a general and ever-

18. *Ibid.,* p. 81.

widening interest in all sorts of psychic phenomena, including spiritualism, astrology, Theosophy, yoga, parapsychology, and so on. Even the modern preoccupation with the physical body is a result of the psychological reassessment of human nature; for the attempt to pass beyond the present level of consciousness through the acceptance of the unconscious brings with it a different conception of the nature and the role of the body. Above all, modern man thirsts for direct physical and spiritual experience. Because everything that the traditional approaches and organizations offer seems lifeless and outworn, instinctively modern man "leaves the trodden paths to explore the by-ways and lanes, just as the man of the Greco-Roman world cast off his defunct Olympian gods and turned to the mystery cults of Asia."[19] Like the Roman religion, today's Western religions have lost, for many, their psychological validity and have become institutions of mere objective ritual. Hence, people now go about trying "on a variety of religious beliefs as if they were Sunday attire, only to lay them aside again like worn-out clothes."[20] Having become bankrupt spiritually, it is not surprising that religious organizations take an increasingly active part in politics; but for the modern man, this only reinforces his doubts and makes religions as suspect as politics.

Clearly, the passionate interest in the various psychological and occult phenomena, in witchcraft, drugs, meditation, and oriental mysticism, is animated by the psychic energy that is no longer invested in the objective world or in the orthodox religions. What modern man seeks in all these cults and practices is *knowledge*. Faith, which is the essence of Western religions, no longer satisfies him. "He wants to *know*—to experience for himself."[21] This is why so many of the sects have a

19. *Ibid.*, p. 92.
20. *Ibid.*, p. 83.
21. *Ibid.*, p. 84.

"scientific" veneer or involve immediately given experiences. Even such things as the revival of "speaking in tongues" in some Christian sects are symptomatic of this change in orientation. Modern man wants original experience and not assumptions, and his approach is as sceptical and as ruthless as that of the Buddha, who swept aside all the Hindu gods so that he might reach that original experience which alone is convincing. The popular fascination with all these strange psychological and religious phenomena may seem like a sign of decadence, but it may also be a sign of rejuvenation: in significant ways, the contemporary situation is reminiscent of the first century of the Christian era, and we are witnessing a fundamental spiritual change in the Western world. "It is the more noteworthy because it is rooted in the [lower] social strata, and the more important because it touches those irrational and—as history shows—incalculable psychic forces which transform the life of peoples and civilizations in ways that are unforeseen and unforeseeable."[22] The movement is still below the cultural surface; it finds expression in people from the more obscure levels of society who follow the unconscious proddings of the psyche and are less infected with cultural, academic, and intellectual prejudices.

In 1928 Jung could point to only a handful of Orientalists, a few Buddhist enthusiasts, and a couple of celebrities like Madame Blavatsky and Annie Besant with her Krishnamurti; but even then he thought that these were not mere oddities, but the vanguard of a growing movement. "Sophisticated" intellectuals, he points out, assumed that superstition and astrology were disposed of long before 1928 and could be safely laughed at. Yet, despite universal, "enlightened" education, it seems that "the world has not grown poorer by a single super-

22. *Ibid.*, p. 92.

stition since the days of antiquity," while astrology, "rising out of the social deeps . . . knocks at the doors of the universities from which it was banished some three hundred years ago."[23] Jung feels that it was not pure chance that soon after the enthronement of the Goddess of Reason in Notre Dame there appeared the first Western translation of the *Upanishads*. Nor does he think it an accident that while the West is turning the material world of the East upside down with its superior technology, the East is turning the spiritual world of the West upside down with its superior psychological insights. Both of these developments seem to accord with certain psychological and historical principles: extremes call forth their opposites, and the physically stronger conquerors of a culturally superior people succumb to the influence of the culture they have "conquered."

So far, what the West has taken from the East is still amateurish and mere imitation. And although the East is playing a role in the spiritual changes that are taking place today in the Western world, it is not the geographical or historical East that really matters. For the changes are also the result of the evolution of an Eastern attitude that is basically within us. Jung believes that if this Eastern spirit continues to evolve, it may in time help to subdue what he sees as the boundless lust for prey of the Aryan man. Then, in the near future, "we shall perhaps come to know something of that narrowing of horizons which has grown in the East into dubious quietism, and also something of that stability which human existence acquires when the claims of the spirit become as imperative as the necessities of social life. . . . I do not wish to pass myself off as a prophet," he continues, "but one can hardly attempt to sketch the spiritual problem of modern man without mentioning the longing for rest in a period

23. *Ibid.*, pp. 85 and 87.

of unrest, the longing for security in an age of insecurity. It is from need and distress that new forms of existence arise, and not from idealistic requirements or mere wishes."[24]

Meanwhile, the world in 1928, as afterward, had taken up the American beat—the very opposite of quietism and world-negating resignation. But this can only increase the already existing tension between objective and subjective realities. Since America is at the forefront of Western attitudes, of Western science and technology, and since it lacks the historical anchor of Europe, it is not surprising that the most widespread disillusionment, scepticism, and uncertainty, together with psychological experimentation, upheaval, and unrest are experienced in America. But perhaps, Jung speculates, the general American disorientation is "a last desperate effort to escape the dark sway of natural law, and to wrest a yet greater and more heroic victory of waking consciousness over the sleep of the nations."[25] It is a question only history can answer.

Considering the date of its composition, "The Spiritual Problem of Modern Man" is a most unusual essay. Even ten years ago, it could have been dismissed as only another example of Jung's muddleheadedness and mysticism. Today the news media and every book shop attest to the validity of its predictions.[26] This

24. *Ibid.*, pp. 91–92.
25. *Ibid.*, p. 94.
26. Robert Jay Lifton, who styles himself a psychohistorian, recently has come to see the plight of modern man in terms very similar to those of Jung. Lifton first noted these problems during his studies of postwar Japanese youth, and then observed similar patterns among Chinese and Americans. He found that especially young people today are characterized by frequent and sudden changes in political and religious beliefs and life-styles. Lifton ascribes these psychological convulsions to the same causes as Jung: historical and cultural dislocation; exposure to a plethora of cultural alternatives that remain on a superficial and undigested level; absence of a cultural and individual super-ego; the loss of a stable identity; a sense of freedom and absence of limitations; emphasis

fact adds credence to Jung's contention that he was able to anticipate general social trends on the basis of his cumulative experience with the psychological problems of his individual analysands. It also lends support to two of his basic premises: that the fundamental cultural movements of history are frequently determined more by psychological than by economic or political forces; and that these changes occur first on the individual level and are not the outcome of consciously organized forms coming "from the top."

Modern existentialism was unknown, and Sartre was a university student when Jung first identified the essential existentialist themes: the lack of historical determinism or limitation, the breakdown of values, the total freedom, the sense of absurdity, the responsibility of choosing, the disorientation, doubt, angst, and sense of guilt, the loneliness, and the contrast between the authentic and the pseudomodern man. The existentialist philosophers systematized and intellectualized the psychological experience of the fully conscious modern Western man, and the best among them wrote in a literary and emotional style befitting their experience at the brink of consciousness, where the traditional rules of reason and logic no longer sufficed to describe the reality of man's existence.

Jung alone of the major theorists of depth psychology proposes a general theory that serves to explain some of the more unusual and, in terms of the standard cultural assumptions and

in the society on action, movement, and experimentation; feelings of anxiety and guilt; a spirit of cynicism and mockery; desire for authenticity; and disillusionment with science and technology. In addition, Lifton thinks that the threat of nuclear annihilation has a particularly adverse effect upon the psyche because it undermines the essential need for "symbolic immortality" through nature, children, works of art, and so on. He therefore explains the current concern with ecology and the experimentation with drugs and mysticism as attempts to salvage at least the life of nature and to find immortality through "experiential transcendence." See "Protean Man" in *History and Human Survival* (New York: Vintage, 1971). The book is a collection of essays summarizing Lifton's work during the past decade.

expectations of the day, unforeseeable contemporary psychosocial developments. Orthodox Freudian explanations for the sexually emancipated generation's experimentation with hallucinogenic drugs, its fascination with parapsychology and the occult, and its search for personal religious experience are farfetched and unconvincing; no amount of ingenious stretching of sexual symbolism can make sense of the images produced by hallucinogens. Saying that these developments are a symptom of the longing for a return to the womb, or of an escape from mature responsibility, from the harshness and disappointments of reality, is perhaps a valid description of the motivations involved—but it is not an explanation. Similarly, claiming that these preoccupations are a mass infantile delusion explains nothing.[27]

The developments that Jung describes should have a telling effect on politics. Above all, they will probably lead to a "demystification" of politics. The faith, loyalty, and enthusiasm that until recently men had directed toward the state or placed at the disposal of political movements are slowly being withdrawn. The religious instincts are no longer fully bottled up and diverted to politics, which should, therefore, soon lose its place as the central concern and chief preoccupation of modern man. And the religious interests that are beginning to replace it will be expressed in a more individual and introverted manner than has been the case in the past in the West.

Such a cultural revolution ought to have a salutary effect upon politics. The many conflicts and tensions that have an unconscious and nonpolitical cause will no longer take on a political form, add their fuel to the fires of legitimate political problems, and so distort the political process. The religious and

27. Neither are Marxist formulae particularly helpful; for these developments are hardly the "opium" of the culturally and materially deprived masses or the expected consequences of the growing "contradictions" of a decaying capitalism.

inward orientation should also temper the desire for territorial and economic expansion. Yet such predictions should be made with caution: neither medieval Europe nor the East has been immune to wars and imperialism. There is really no assurance that, having given up on politics, men will not once again revert to religious fanaticisms and wars—a change of outward form that would really change very little. Yet so many things point to the possibility of a change that will be more than just a change in form: the threat of global annihilation, the existence of worldwide communications and cultural exchange, the disillusionment with politics and political ideologies, the scepticism about "progress," science, and materialism, the interest in psychology, the turning inward, and the search for religious experience.

Jung's theory of the stages of life, if extended from the individual to civilization, also tends to show that the coming changes are of a fundamental nature. Having earlier passed through infancy, childhood, and adolescence, Western civilization is now coming to the end of its youth. Youth is devoted to the development of individuality and to concern with procreation, family, material security, and power. Its orientation is external and its actions largely unconscious and conditioned by the essential needs of nature. The stage of maturity, which Western civilization is now entering, is devoted to the development of an inner life and the cultivation of cultural interests. Its orientation is inward and its actions consciously determined and guided by cultural aspirations. Ideally, therefore, evolution is from the pleasure to the reality principle, from extroversion to introversion, from nature to culture. With the ego now firmly established, individuality and consciousness differentiated from the group, and the emotions deliberately cultivated, the mature individual or civilization is ready to sustain a new psychological development—the evolution of the Self, the integration of the conscious and the unconscious into a new psychic totality.

8

The Future of Man

Thirty years after writing "The Spiritual Problem of Modern Man," Jung once again turned to the question of the future development of mankind. The immediate reason for his concern was the flying saucer phenomenon. For ten years he had collected data on the occurrences, and in 1958 he published a book entitled *Flying Saucers: A Modern Myth of Things Seen in the Skies.* His conclusion concerning the nature of flying saucers concurs with that of Edward J. Ruppelet, head of the United States Air Force investigations of UFO reports: *"Something is seen, but one doesn't know what."*[1] It is this conclusion that makes the saucers an interesting problem for psychology.

On the basis of his examination of the data surrounding the phenomenon, Jung contends that flying saucers are a rare variation of a visionary rumor, closely related to such collective visions as those of the Crusaders during the siege of Jerusalem, the troops at Mons in the First World War, or the Catholics gathered at Fatima. The origins of the rumor may be explained by two hypotheses: an objectively real, physical event provides

1. *Flying Saucers: A Modern Myth of Things Seen in the Sky,* volume 10, p. 312.

125

the foundation for the accompanying myth; or an archetype creates the visionary experience—in this case, a physical object could trigger the vision—and gives rise to the rumor.[2] In either case, a projection occurs, and projections have a psychic cause.

Jung thinks that "the basis for this kind of rumour is an *emotional tension* having its cause in a situation of collective distress or danger, or in a vital psychic need."[3] Since the rumor is worldwide, the emotional tension must similarly be more or less universal, although, interestingly enough, the United States leads the rest of the world in UFO sightings and reports. Jung maintains that such abnormal projections occur only when there is severe opposition and tension between conscious attitudes and unconscious contents. The conscious mind does not acknowledge the unconscious contents and therefore cannot integrate them into the personality. The unconscious, then, is forced to resort to unusual methods in order to dispose of its pent-up energy; hence there arise unexpected and apparently unaccountable opinions, beliefs, illusions, visions, and so on. The sighting of a UFO is frequently reported by a witness who "is above suspicion because he was never distinguished for his lively imagination or credulousness, but, on the contrary, for his cool judgment and critical reason."[4] In such instances, the unconscious has had to resort to the drastic measure of projecting a vision in order to dispose of its contents and have them perceived.

In general, therefore, the UFO phenomenon is valuable from a psychological and a historical point of view, because it provides an excellent example of how a legend, or a living myth, is

2. *Ibid.*, p. 313. To these two causal hypotheses, Jung adds a third possibility, that of synchronicity, that is, an acausal meaningful coincidence; he does not elaborate on this hypothesis, however. See his "Synchronicity: An Acausal Connecting Principle," in volume 8 of the *Collected Works.*

3. *Flying Saucers: A Modern Myth of Things Seen in the Sky,* volume 10, p. 319.

4. *Ibid.*, p. 320.

formed. It also discloses how, during times of widespread disorientation and stress, a miraculous tale springs up about the
coming intervention of extraterrestrial beings or "heavenly"
powers. For visionary projections in the skies are not new—a
good deal of astrology, Jung thinks, was based on unconscious
and probably synchronistic projections of emotion-laden images
in the night sky—and have occurred at various times in history;
but their form, content, and interpretation have always expressed the needs and concurred with the Weltanschauung of
the period in which they took place. Thus the tale that arose of
the imminent end of the world through divine intervention
during the confused transition era of the time of Christ would be
unacceptable to most contemporary men. But the "scientific,"
technological interpretation of the modern visions as flying
saucers makes them acceptable even for Marxists—the popular
interest in flying saucers in the Soviet Union is considerable.
Nevertheless, in both the Christian and modern legends, the ex-
pectation of either destruction or salvation by a superior power is
a vital element of the myth and illustrates the similarities in the
hopes and fears of the times. *Chariots of the Gods?* by Erich Von
Daniken, which explains all earlier religious myths as having
their origins in man's encounters with superior beings from
outer space, is an excellent example of the pseudoscientific,
semireligious treatment of the flying saucer myth; not incidentally, the book has been an extraordinary international best
seller.

Jung thinks that the contents of a vision can be subjected to
the same principles of interpretation as dreams. The images in
both visions and dreams are symbolic representations of unconscious processes. In some cases, the UFOs are reported to be
oblong; here the phallic comparison and its analogy with other
ancient symbols of the divinity is appropriate. But most flying

saucers are round in form and are analogous to the symbol of totality known as the mandala. The mandala is a symbol of wholeness, of order; its function is to organize and embrace the psychic totality and to regulate and reorder chaotic states. In earlier periods, spherical images like saucers might have been interpreted as representations of gods or souls; in contemporary terms, Jung defines them as symbolic representations of the *Self*—by which he does not mean the ego, "but the totality composed of the conscious *and* the unconscious."[5] The mandala is an archetype of the Self. And since archetypes have an instinctual or physiological base, the fact that some of the images composing UFO visions and rumors also have a sexual—round-female, oblong-male—interpretation indicates that the powerful sexual instinct has a share in the constellation of the phenomenon. But this is to be expected of a genuine symbol; it should not only express man's conscious, technological, or philosophical fantasies, but strike deep into his animal nature as well: "It must affect and express the whole man."[6]

Apparently the worldwide social, political, religious, and cultural turmoil and the modern scission between the conscious and the unconscious parts of the psyche have given rise to a situation that begs for the imposition of some harmony and order. The desire to put an end to the external and conscious state of chaos, and the inner tension between the separated psychic opposites generate the necessary energy for the "uniting symbol" to appear. At first the symbol is unconscious and therefore easily projected—hence, the flying saucers. Because the symbol is collective and archetypal in nature, the projection carries with it numinous and mythical powers which are responsible for the spread and the persistence of the rumor. Since the mandala is a

5. *Ibid.*, pp. 326-27.
6. *Ibid.*, p. 350.

symbol of order and plays the main role in uniting apparently irreconcilable opposites, it is well-suited to compensate for the disorder and the split-mindedness of our age.

States of severe social and psychological disorder and tension always evoke the need for a "savior," whether on the individual or the collective level. In the past, the archetype of the Self created the image of a divine-human personality—Elijah, Christ, Buddha, Khidr—who became the savior and the symbol of self-realization. Today, probably reflecting the further evolution of the psyche, the archetype of the Self is projected in the more abstract symbol of the mandala. Its appearance at the present time, Jung asserts, demonstrates that individuation (Jung's term for self-realization, for the integration of the conscious and the unconscious through the Self—a new psychic entity replacing the ego as the center of the personality) is the alternative to mass-mindedness, and hence the great challenge that faces our civilization.[7] Jung attempts to construct a convincing case for his interpretation with discussions of known dreams about UFOs, which disclose how UFOs are understood by the unconscious; of certain modern paintings, which he thinks express the dominant trends of the age; and of earlier historical reports of mobile round objects in the sky.

Jung states, in the Introduction to his book, that the saucer visions and rumors seem to him so significant that he feels "compelled, as once before [in the 1936 essay on Wotan] when events of fateful consequence were brewing for Europe, to sound a note of warning."[8] He thinks the phenomenon is a manifestation of "changes in the constellation of psychic dominants, of the archetypes, or 'gods' as they used to be called, which bring about, or accompany, long-lasting transformations

7. The challenge is two-pronged, for the need for a savior and for a new ordering myth can easily produce a new mass-mindedness, as the case of Germany and Hitler illustrates.
8. *Flying Saucers: A Modern Myth of Things Seen in the Sky,* volume 10, p. 311.

of the collective psyche."[9] The changes seem to correspond to the passage from one astrological Platonic month to another: the earth is presently leaving Pisces and entering Aquarius. Jung admits that such reflections are "exceedingly unpopular and even come perilously close to those turbid fantasies which becloud the minds of world-reformers and other interpreters of 'signs and portents.' "[10] But he claims that he is willing to risk his reputation for reliability and capacity for scientific judgment in order to undertake the task of examining and setting forth the possible psychological consequences of the change that he foresees.

Whenever archetypal forces are mobilized on a wide scale, dangerous as well as beneficial possibilities result; for archetypes determine the psychic attitudes and social behavior of the individual and the collective, and every archetype contains both positive and negative features. If the positive contents are not permitted conscious expression, but are repressed, their energy passes over to the negative aspects of the archetype; then it is only a matter of time before it creates serious and uncontrollable disturbances in the psyche and in society. Only a consciousness of the archetypes and a knowledge of their characteristic features can ensure that their beneficial contents are given objective expression, while their harmful aspects are disarmed and controlled. "It depends on us whether we help coming events to birth by understanding them, and reinforce their healing effect, or whether we repress them with our prejudices, narrow-mindedness and ignorance, thus turning their effect into its opposite, into poison and destruction."[11]

Once again Jung concludes that the result, for good or ill, depends on the understanding and the ethical decisions of the individual. The general psychological constellation disclosed by

9. *Ibid.*
10. *Ibid.*, p. 312.
11. *Ibid.*, p. 388.

the saucer phenomenon strengthens Jung's conviction that the tasks and the problems that presently confront man are not amenable to collective recipes and nostrums. On the contrary, what is called for is individual resistance to the collective pull of the archetype of unity and order, and a conscious personal acceptance of its thrust for individual integration and self-realization. Needless to say, it is impossible to force a "good" solution upon men. Such a solution in any case is valid only when it is associated with a natural process of development, and the principle upon which any individual builds his life must be generally acceptable—otherwise, it lacks that feeling of natural morality that man, as a social being, finds indispensable for his activity. But if Jung's interpretation of the flying saucer business is even partially correct, such a natural process of development and such a generally accepted principle—a principle directed toward a more integrated and peaceful individual and social life—are now upon us. Nevertheless, these developments, if they remain unrecognized, unconscious, and undirected, can easily become distorted. It must not be forgotten that similar archetypal forces for unity and order were activated not long ago in Germany; the opposite of order is chaos, the opposite of individualism is mass-mindedness, and the opposite of self-realization is self-destruction. The external and internal forces capable of moving in either direction are now present, and the possibility of either imminent.

In sum, what Jung is saying is that the currently energized archetype of the Self may be projected onto an individual or a myth; it may take on a personal or an abstract representation; the response to it may be individual or collective; and its consequences may be positive or negative, both for the individual and for the society. Salvationist, millennarian myths and ideologies are a common inheritance of mankind, always ready to be put to use. Similarly, individuals who are willing to take on the flattering projection of "savior" are easily found. When the need arises, it is then merely a question of rallying around a myth that accords with the general attitudes of the time or of focusing upon a suitable individual. To the extent that people today have become disillusioned with political ideologies and leaders, these are no longer capable of carrying such projections.

The New Left represents a case in point. Politics was the arena in which many members of the generation that came of age in the sixties placed their hopes for a utopian future. But that realm proved to be much more conservative and intractable than had been expected, and the New Left movement was not amenable to the long-term organizational work necessary to achieve political changes. The extreme optimism turned to excessive despair. Some withdrew; others grudgingly joined the "establishment"; a few turned to terroism; some turned inward; and others, after a period of apathy and disorientation shifted their aspirations to the religious sphere. Hence the new movement, drawing on the same New Left constituency, gathers at the feet of the adolescent-god Maharaj Ji. It is noteworthy, but in view of our discussion not surprising, that at the movement's November 1973 meeting—billed as Millennium '73—in the Houston Astrodome, a space was left in the parking lot for an expected landing by UFOs.

The Divine Light Mission, as this reincarnation of the New Left is called, and the thousands of other sects sprouting around various gurus attest to the pressure of the archetype of the Self as it seeks outward expression. Jung calls attention to this fact and asks that it be consciously acknowledged. Otherwise, he warns, such movements will continue to grow, as they do now, in an unconscious and undirected way. Individuals will be sucked in, hardly understanding what is happening to them. And the usual problems associated with a mass of men possessed by the unconscious will follow. Then it is only a matter of time before one of these cults turns into a dynamic, destructive movement reminiscent of the political mass movements of this century or of the millennarian movements of the Middle Ages. The positive alternative is for men to individually accept the currently given opportunity to achieve a new unity and a new relationship between the conscious and the unconscious. What such a change in the psyche would mean for the political and social future of man, however, is still impossible to predict.

9

Jung and Freud

I have no intention in this chapter of undertaking a full-scale comparison of Jung and Freud.[1] The comparison is limited to those theories and ideas that have implications for political theory and practice. The task is not as easy as it may sound, for the differences between the two men in basic attitude and method are reminiscent of the differences between Plato and Aristotle, or St. Augustine and St. Thomas Aquinas. Freud writes in a direct, systematic style and thinks along rational, positivistic, causal lines. Jung writes in a more intuitive, impressionistic way and considers reason, positivism, and causality inadequate for the description of the nature and the functions of the psyche. Both the influences on his intellectual development and his personal attitude toward the world hark back to the Romantic period and its reaction against the rationalism of the Enlightenment. And his scientific outlook, although empirical,

1. For a thorough comparison of their psychological theories, see Liliane Frey-Rohn, *From Freud to Jung: A Comparative Study of the Psychology of the Unconscious* (New York: G. P. Putnam's Sons, 1975).

is more in tune with the relativism of the science of the twentieth century, particularly physics. Freud, on the other hand, is an adherent of the Enlightenment, a believer in the efficacy of reason, and an advocate of the positivistic methods of nineteenth-century science. Consequently, a coherent exposition of Freud's theories is not particularly difficult; but with Jung, every central concept is treated in a variety of ways in different contexts, so that in the end the question remains open. A presentation of Jung's ideas, therefore, always involves some creative interpositions and elaborations, as well as the possibility of misinterpretation and distortion. Finally, both men were pioneers in an unexplored realm and their ideas changed and evolved over a period of time. As a result, their writings often contain partially formed, abandoned, and even contradictory notions, so that some care must be exercised in any exposition and comparison of their ideas. Despite all these difficulties, however, I think that a comparison is possible, and, for the sake of a broader understanding of human attitudes and behavior, desirable.

Freud's writings on politics, like those of Jung, are peripheral to his central concerns. He is, however, somewhat more systematic in the presentation of his political ideas. The writings devoted primarily to politics include: *Totem and Taboo* (1913), *Group Psychology and the Analysis of the Ego* (1921), *Civilization and Its Discontents* (1930), and two essays, "Thoughts for the Times on War and Death" (1915) and "Why War?" (1933). The recently published study of *Thomas Woodrow Wilson* on which Freud collaborated with W. C. Bullitt in the early 1930s does disservice to Freud both stylistically and conceptually. It adds nothing to an understanding of his psychological and political concepts, with the exception, perhaps, of demonstrating the limitations of psychoanalysis.

TOTEM, TABOO, AND MANA

Totem and Taboo was Freud's first attempt to apply his psychoanalytic method to sociological and political issues, and he notes in the Preface to the book that it offers a "methodological contrast" to Jung's reliance on materials from social psychology for the solution of problems in individual psychology.[2] Freud agrees with Wilhelm Wundt that taboos are the oldest human code of laws and that acts forbidden by taboos or laws are acts "which many men have a natural propensity to commit."[3] But he rejects Wundt's thesis that taboos stem from the primitive's belief in a daemonic power lying concealed within men, animals, and objects, and his fear of rousing that power through improper treatment or attitude. Using his psychoanalytical experience, Freud discovers analogies between taboo usages and the symptoms of obsessional neurosis, and, on the basis of these insights, states that taboos originally arose from prohibitions of instinctual desires and acts, prohibitions imposed violently upon a generation of primitive men by a previous generation. This hypothesis explains man's ambivalent attitude toward what a taboo forbids; for instinctively, and after the imposition of the taboo, unconsciously, there is nothing men would like more than to violate the taboo. The magical power attributed to the taboo as well as the fascination that it evokes are products of its capacity for temptation and for arousing instinctual and unconscious drives. Hence the necessity of formidable conscious resistances—the sacredness of the taboo, the repeated and emphatic injunctions not to violate it, and the severe punishment when it is disobeyed. At first, Freud believes,

2. Sigmund Freud, *The Standard Edition of the Complete Psychological Works of Sigmund Freud,* 24 vols. (London: The Hogarth Press, 1955), volume 13, p. xiii. Hereafter referred to as the *Standard Edition.*

3. *Ibid.*, p. 123. Freud approvingly quotes J. G. Frazer to the effect that taboos and laws only forbid "men to do what their instincts incline them to do." The reference is to J. G. Frazer's *Totemism and Exogamy* (1910), volume 4, p. 97.

taboos were transmitted through parental and social authority, but in later generations it is possible that "they may have become 'organized' as an inherited psychical endowment." [4]

The oldest and the most important taboos appear to be the two basic laws of totemism: "not to kill the totem animal and to avoid sexual intercourse with members of the totem clan of the opposite sex."[5] Hence, these must also be the oldest and the most powerful drives thwarted by society. In order to account for the origin of these two taboos, Freud has recourse to Darwin's thesis that, like the higher apes, men initially lived in small groups or hordes. Each of these "primal hordes," composed of a harem of females and their offspring, was ruled by a physically powerful male, or patriarch, who jealously reserved for himself sexual access to all the females, driving off other males, including his own sons.

> One day the brothers who had been driven out came together, killed and devoured their father and so made an end of the patriarchal horde. United, they had the courage to do and succeeded in doing what would have been impossible for them individually. (Some cultural advance, perhaps, command over some new weapon, had given them a sense of superior strength.) Cannibal savages as they were, it goes without saying that they devoured their victim as well as killing him. The violent primal father had doubtless been the feared and envied model of each one of the company of brothers: and in the act of devouring him they accomplished their identification with him, and each one of them acquired a portion of his strength. The totem meal, which is perhaps mankind's earliest festival, would thus be a repetition and a commemoration of this memorable and criminal deed, which was the beginning of so many things—of social organization, of moral restrictions and of religion. [6]

4. *Ibid.*, p. 31.
5. *Ibid.*, p. 32.
6. *Ibid.*, pp. 141–42. In chapter 10 of *Group Psychology*, where Freud returns to a treatment of the primal horde, he speculates that it was the sons' homosexuality that provided them with the sense of unity that was needed. See volume 18 of the *Standard Edition*, p. 135.

Supposedly, the same event occurred within numerous primal hordes, and once united, the brothers of one horde could easily overpower other patriarchs, or wage war against the united brothers of another horde.

The brothers had ambivalent feelings toward their father—they both loved and feared, admired and hated him. Once they had killed him, devoured him, enjoyed his women, and so identified themselves with him, remorse and guilt set in. They therefore "revoked their deed by forbidding the killing of the totem, the substitute for their father; and they renounced its fruits by resigning their claim to the women who had now been set free."[7] Here, then, is the origin of totemism and of its two central taboos—not to kill the totem animal, and not to have sexual intercourse with a woman of the same totem. Interestingly enough, the two taboos with which, according to Freud, human morality had its start, coincide with the repressed wishes characteristic of the Oedipus complex—the son's desire to "kill" his father and "marry" his mother; the theory that the totem animal is a substitute for the father is substantiated for Freud by the results of his psychoanalytic work with male children.

The renunciation of sexual intercourse with the women of the same totem, the source of the incest taboo, brought with it certain practical advantages, aside from the one of avoiding the dangers of inbreeding. Each one of the brothers would have liked to take his father's place; by freeing the women, they avoided the fratricidal struggle that would otherwise have occurred[8] and so preserved their unity and their strength and instituted the fraternal community in which civilization began.

7. *Ibid.*, p. 143.

8. In *Group Psychology* Freud adds: "None of the group of victors could take his place, or, if one of them did, the battles began afresh, until they understood that they must all renounce their father's heritage" (Volume 18 of the *Standard Edition*, p. 135).

The patricide and the resulting taboo against killing the totem animal, on the other hand, initiated various religious attitudes, injunctions, and practices. Here is the "original sin," the sin against the Father, and the sense of guilt, remorse, and shame. Here, too, is the reason for the desire to appease the Father by "deferred" obedience to His wishes, and for the covenant not to repeat the evil act in return for His protection and indulgence. The patricide also explains the bipolarity of the emotions associated with religion—the sense of guilt and the feeling of triumph.

Finally, the affectionate feelings among the brothers that were responsible for their victory over the father "found expression in the sanctification of the blood tie, in the emphasis upon the solidarity of all life within the same clan."[9] To the prohibition against killing the totem was added the prohibition against fratricide, and from that it was a short step to the universalized moral admonition, "Thou shalt not kill." And so, Freud summarizes: "Society was now based on complicity in the common crime; religion was based on the sense of guilt and the remorse attaching to it; while morality was based partly on the exigencies of this society and partly on the penance demanded by the sense of guilt."[10]

In the concluding pages of *Totem and Taboo* Freud discusses two possible difficulties with respect to his thesis. He admits that his argument rests on the presupposition of "the existence of a collective mind, in which mental processes occur just as they do in the mind of an individual."[11] For he assumes that the original sense of guilt remains operative in generations thousands of years removed from the actual act and even from the knowledge of the act. Thus there must be some form of collective

9. Freud, *Standard Edition*, volume 13, p. 146.
10. *Ibid.*
11. *Ibid.*, p. 157.

mind which permits psychological processes to be continued and developed from one generation to the next; in fact, social psychology would be impossible if each generation had to acquire its attitudes to life anew. The nature of the collective mind, however, and the process by which mental attitudes are passed on still require investigation. As an opening contribution, Freud offers two suggestions: the possibility of the "inheritance of psychical dispositions," which nevertheless require some stimulus in the life of the individual to be activated; and the possibility of an "unconscious understanding" by the new generation of even concealed and distorted mental processes, "customs, ceremonies and dogmas left behind by the original relation to the father."[12]

The second difficulty derives from psychoanalytical experience: in the majority of cases a neurotic's sense of guilt is based not on an actual event but on a psychic event, on psychic reality. Freud notes that such neurotic overvaluation of psychical acts or events is also true of primitive men, and he therefore thinks it possible that "the mere hostile *impulse* against the father, the mere existence of a wishful *phantasy* of killing and devouring him, would have been enough to produce the moral reaction that created totemism and taboo."[13] But he insists that for both the neurotic and the primitive, historical reality has some share in the psychic response and argues that this must be particularly true of primitives, who unlike neurotics are uninhibited in their actions: for primitive men, "thought passes directly into action"; consequently, in the words of Goethe's Faust, "In the beginning was the Deed."[14]

Jung has no quarrel with Freud's contention in the Preface of *Totem and Taboo* that Jung and his followers rely on materials

12. *Ibid.*, pp. 158–59.
13. *Ibid.*, pp. 159–60.
14. *Ibid.*, p. 161.

from social psychology for the solution of problems posed by individual psychology. Instead, he takes Freud to task for putting the cart before the horse and basing his theories of social psychology on the psychology of the individual. As Jung sees it, Freud remained essentially a psychoanalyst working with individuals and their problems. It was not in his line to investigate the foundations of psychological knowledge, which would have involved historical research, and he simply skipped comparative psychology, moving into a conjectural and highly uncertain prehistory of the human psyche. "In so doing he lost the ground from under his feet, for he would not let himself be taught by the findings of ethnologists and historians, but transferred the insights he had gained from modern neurotics during consulting hours directly to the broad field of primitive psychology."[15] Jung thinks it is obvious that the psyche is not restricted to the "narrow subjective sphere of the individual personality but, over and above that [it also has roots] in collective psychic phenomena of whose existence Freud was aware, at least in principle, as his concept of the 'superego' shows."[16]

Jung does not think much of Freud's analogy between taboo usages and the symptoms of obsessional neurosis, nor of the conclusion that taboos must be derived from prohibitions imposed upon instinctual drives. Jung himself exerts little effort to discover the origin of taboos; he simply conjectures that they stem from what he calls the typical superstitious fears of primitive man, fears that arise independently of any prohibitions.[17] He does note, on the basis of the anthropological findings of Levy-Bruhl, that the various taboos seem to correspond with areas of the psyche that, if activated, might lead to a "loss of soul," that is, possession or going berserk; since the

15. *Flying Saucers: A Modern Myth of Things Seen in the Skies,* volume 10, p. 349.
16. *Ibid.,* p. 348.
17. "Psychoanalysis and Neurosis," volume 4, p. 247.

primitive psyche easily succumbs to emotional contagion, epidemics of possession and running amok can follow with disastrous social and personal consequences. Even fairly ordinary emotions, in the immature or poorly differentiated psyche, can produce considerable loss of consciousness. Hence, taboos and rituals, whose aim is to bring about a separation of subject and object and thereby raise consciousness and allow for deliberate behavior, surround all unknown, exceptional, emotionally charged, and hence fearsome, events. But fear, whether of external objects, exceptional states, or the "loss of soul," is not something that is consciously determined. Consequently, Jung concludes that it must have been "the evolutionary instinct peculiar to man, which distinguishes him so radically from all other animals...[that] forced upon him countless taboos, among them the incest taboo."[18]

Freud, in his discussion of taboos, also attempts to explain the manifestation of mana, that "mysterious power" that seems to be inherent in all taboo conditions, persons, and things. He ascribes it to a projection of the libidinal energy that is repressed by taboo prohibitions. Up to a point, Jung agrees. But Jung refuses to limit the projection to repressed instinctual drives. He thinks that the projection of any important psychic component produces a mana-condition, and, moreover, that there are mana-personalities who are impressive in their own right and not because of projection.[19] No doubt the same could be said of certain objects and events. But awe-inspiring personalities, objects, and events do invariably provide a "hook" for projections, so that the situation is never one-sided, and projection always plays a role in the experience of mana.

Following F. R. Lehmann's study *Mana* (1922), Jung defines

18. *Symbols of Transformation,* volume 5, pp. 418–19.
19. "Archaic Man," volume 10, p. 69.

mana as "the extraordinarily potent," and traces it to the primitive religious notion that there exists a "universal magical power about which everything revolves."[20] However, there is nothing especially divine about it, and it is responsible for both extraordinary and ordinary processes of nature, among the latter, fertility and growth. While associated with human qualities that surpass the ordinary, such as magical knowledge, it also has to do with general health, strength, power, and prestige. It attaches itself to persons and things, is not fixed, but highly mobile, and can have either beneficial or harmful effects. Eventually it becomes equivalent to the idea of soul, spirit, or atman, and serves as the earliest form of the concept of God. Jung regards it as the prototype of the general concept of energy and of his own notion of psychic energy. He maintains that the experience of energy, like that of time, has been impressed on the brain for aeons and therefore is an *a priori,* intuitive idea—an archetype. An an archetype it structures the apprehension of the reaction to inner and outer reality, and it carries with it a "libido investment," or a "feeling tone," so that its activation gives rise to emotional reactions and objective behavior that even today seem mysterious and inexplicable. It lies ready in the unconscious of every collective and individual psyche, and its manifestation has been called by various names. Freud called it libido. Modern sociology refers to it as charisma, and the so-called counterculture dubs it vibrations or "vibes."[21]

THE DEVELOPMENT OF CULTURE

In the first chapter of this book we explored Jung's conception of

20. *Two Essays,* volume 7, p. 231 and p. 67.
21. The early Romans called this energy "numen." Jung follows Rudolf Otto's *The Idea of the Holy* and uses the English derivation of the term as an adjective to describe the possession of mana: that which has mana is "numinous" or has "numinosity."

the origin of society from a purely psychological standpoint, using libido as the pivotal concept. Here, where a comparison with Freud is the aim, it is necessary to approach the problem from other directions—mythological and anthropological—in which the notion of incest plays the central role.

Jung agrees with Freud that the longing for the mother, for a return to the source from which we come, and the physical impossibility of satisfying this yearning have something to do with the origin of consciousness and society. In order to shed light on the problem, Jung turns to mythology, which he, like Freud, regards as the symbolic projection of the psychic experiences of mankind. He thinks that the various creation myths are revealing in this respect, for he finds that they all posit some form of all-embracing unity at the beginning of time. That unity is represented variously as the Egyptian Heavenly Serpent that bites its own tail (the uroboros); as the Chinese *t'ai chi*—a round container of all opposites; as the philosophical World Egg; as the alchemical *rotundum;* or as primeval hermaphroditic beings like the Hindu Purusha, Plato's Original Man, and Adam, from whose body Eve was formed. The act of creation involves the subdivision and separation into opposites of the original whole. The separation is pictured as violent, painful, and even as unnatural or sinful. It is here that "the 'longing for the mother,' the nostalgia for the source from which we sprang,"[22] has its beginning. Jung insists that the need is not primarily physical or sexual, and it does not have to do with the actual womb. Subdivision and separation and attempts at reunification are universal chemical and organic processes; the body and the psyche, as products of physical and organic evolution, express desires and longings that transcend the purely personal and human. This is why for man, who is capable of giving symbolic expression to his

22. *Two Essays,* volume 7, p. 167.

needs and drives, whether conscious or unconscious, the desire for a return to the primeval unity takes on a "spiritual" or religious aspect.[23]

Jung thus argues that the religious instinct is as old as mankind—it could be described as a "psychic instinct"—and "the making of a religion or the formation of symbols is just as important an interest of the primitive mind as the satisfaction of [any other] instinct."[24] No murder of a primal father was necessary for religious attitudes, symbols, and practices to appear, and to reduce symbols that deal with cosmological themes to purely personal or literal terms is doing violence to their origin and to the underlying reality that they try to express. Moreover, since religion or "spirit" has an organically instinctual and psychologically archetypal base, a conceptualization that dismisses the religious instinct as an infantile illusion—as Freud's does—is false, and therapeutically, as well as sociologically, harmful. In this connection, Jung states that he does not hold himself "responsible for the fact that man has, always and everywhere, spontaneously developed a religious function, and that the human psyche from time immemorial has been shot through with religious feelings and ideas."[25] He maintains that he has no particular interest in theology but is simply recognizing an empirical fact.

Creation is a two-stage affair that is often collapsed into one: life begins in the World Egg, the uroboros, the womb; already

23. Church fathers who derive the term "religion" from the Latin *religare*, to bind again, could have "made use" of this psychological fact. Jung, however, thinks the more likely derivation is from *religere*, to go through again, think over, recollect, and that this is closer to the idea of a symbolic, spiritual return (*Symbols of Transformation*, volume 5, p. 429).

24. "On Psychic Energy," volume 8, p. 58. By "instinct" Jung simply means any involuntary impulsion toward certain activities; he therefore regards all psychic processes whose energies are not under conscious control as "instinctive." For a more complete definition, see below, pp. 178–80.

25. "Freud and Jung: Contrasts," volume 4, p. 339.

within it the first subdivisions and separations occur, but they continue to exist in an undifferentiated, interrelated state. It is the second stage of creation that brings about the separation into opposites, clear distinctions, order, and separate consciousness.

The return to the womb, to the source of life, is one way of overcoming all estrangement, including the cleavage into opposites that follows the emergence from the original unity. It is a much more fundamental drive, as well as an immeasurably more difficult task, than the reunification of the opposites. The drive for a return to the original condition is the death instinct on the physical level and the death archetype on the psychological.[26] As the death instinct, the drive to return to the source of life "strives" for the gradual decomposition of the body, a return to its original chemical state. As the death archetype, it endeavors to dissolve individuality and consciousness in the "sea" of the collective unconscious. Both the physical and psychological processes are integral parts of life and are expressed in various symbolic forms: burial of the dead, Jonah's sojourn in the belly of the whale, immersion in water during baptism, and so on. The contemplation of the mandala, as a symbol of the unified Self, is also a return to the all-encompassing wholeness of the womb. And like every psychological submergence in the collective unconscious, it is accompanied by depression and an eclipse of the ego.

The paradox, of course, is that the beginning and the end of individual life meet at the same point. One passes into the other, so that the urge for extinction is at the same time an urge for immortality, for a new birth. This is why men have always connected the two, and why they bury their dead, returning them to

26. This is not the same as the Freudian death instinct, which is linked with aggression, destruction, and violence.

the womb of the eternally living Mother Earth. How literally this was taken can be surmised from the fact that in Neolithic times, and in many later primitive societies, the corpse is buried in a fetal position.

Nevertheless the longing for a return to the womb is balanced by a fear of dissolution and extinction. Thus a tension is set up between the fear of life and of death, between the urge for individual differentiation and for collective unity. In mythology, the Hero, having purposely exposed "himself to the danger of being devoured by the monster of the maternal abyss,"[27] is victorious only if he succeeds in conquering the monster; in psychological terms he achieves an individual victory over the attraction of the collective psyche. Identification with the collective psyche and submersion in it is the common, unheroic way of achieving a return to the womb, of gaining a sense of unity, immortality, and peace.

The origin of the instinct for incest and the incest archetype is found in the second stage of creation, the separation of the opposites. Sexuality, in its first manifestations, takes on an incestuous character because it is tainted by the primary urge for the self-contained primeval condition, and because it moves to overcome the opposites at the closest point of separation, where it is felt most intensely. The instinct, therefore, can be traced in the physical attraction between mother and son, father and daughter; the archetype is manifested in the incestuous propagation of the gods and the similar prerogatives of their earthly counterparts, kings and heroes. Jung states that the problem of incest has never been fully conscious and that man has usually projected it and attempted to solve it outside the psyche. In the modern era, like so many other archetypes denied symbolic expression in ritual, it returned to the unconscious where it

27. *Two Essays,* volume 7, p. 168.

regressed to its instinctual base and in this form was discovered by depth psychology. Jung thinks, however, that this may be a prelude to a conscious recognition of the drive, which psychologically is felt as a need for a union with one's own being, for the integration of the conscious and the unconscious. Self-realization or individuation are modern terms for this process.

In his *History of the Psychoanalytic Movement* (1914), Freud discusses the two major dissenters from his views, Adler and Jung. He states that although Adler's theories are patently false, they are nevertheless more important than Jung's, because they are at least consistent, coherent, and still based on the theory of instincts. Jung's modification, on the other hand, loosens the connections between the instincts and the rest of life's phenomena. Moreover, Freud writes, Jung's point of view is so "obscure, unintelligible, and confused" as to make it impossible to take a stand against it: "Wherever one lays hold of anything, one must be prepared to hear that one has misunderstood it, and one cannot see how to arrive at a correct understanding."[28] In a way, Freud's lament is valid, for, as I have tried to indicate at the beginning of this chapter, the attitudes and methods of the two men are grounded in radically different experiences of the world.

As Freud sees it, Jung traced in detail how the sexual notions originating in the family complex and in the desire for incest make their way to the highest ethical and religious ideas of mankind. Freud sees nothing in this procedure that is contrary to the expectations of psychoanalysis; in fact, he finds Jung's work an impressive study of the sublimation of erotic instinctual forces into strivings that can no longer be called erotic. He claims that in dreams and neuroses one can see how these sublimations are regressively dissolved back to their erotic source; but this is "sexualizing" ethics and religion, and Freud

28. Freud, *Standard Edition*, volume 14, p. 60.

thinks that Jung and his followers were simply too timid to face the storm of indignation that this "discovery" produced. Since the connection between the Oedipus complex and religion or ethics is undeniable, Freud believed Jung simply gave the complexes an anagogic meaning from the start, thereby making them useful for abstract thought. Sexual libido was replaced by an abstruse and undefinable concept of energy, and the Oedipus complex was given only a "symbolic" meaning, so that, for example, the father who is killed in the Oedipus myth is represented as an "inner" father. And since a study of early childhood is likely to bring up the original and undisguised meaning of these complexes, Jung made it a therapeutic rule to direct as little attention as possible to the past and to concentrate on the patient's current difficulties.

For his part, Jung asserts that because of his preoccupation with the Oedipus complex and his rationalistic-sexual orientation, Freud turned that complex into a primal cause and misunderstood its true import. Jung thinks that Freud came upon the idea when he encountered serious problems in trying to derive all symbolic psychic materials from once conscious contents. He therefore went as far back as possible in the life of the individual and so hit upon an uncommonly numinous idea, the archetype of incest.[29] Jung claims that much of Freud's dogmatic rigidity can be ascribed to the fact that he succumbed to the numinous effect of this primal image. Its numinosity so colored his thinking that he proceeded to derive all of modern man's psychological problems and all symbolism, past and present, from primal incest. As for the future, he reportedly once asked Jung, "I only wonder what neurotics will do . . . when it is generally known what their symbols mean."[30]

29. Only much later did Freud pick up its corollary, the death archetype.
30. "The Philosophical Tree," volume 13, p. 302.

Jung briefly traces the history of the incest archetype in order to account for its contemporary fate. He sees it as the central theme in the problem of the union of opposites that has plagued mankind for centuries. Usually men have tried to solve the problem in a religious form, relying on theriomorphic or sexual symbolism. With the ascent of rationalism the problem was adopted by philosophy, with Hegel's representing the most comprehensive endeavor. But with the concurrent eclipse of the meaning of religious symbolism for most men, the archetype's libido regressed to its instinctual base and remained there until the Enlightenment advanced far enough for "sexuality" to be mentioned in scientific conversation. Then the sexuality of the unconscious was taken with utmost seriousness, elevated to a sort of religious dogma, and fanatically defended; for as so often happens, once repressed contents of the unconscious come to the surface, their energy and fascination is such that they almost overpower the conscious mind. In Jung's opinion, these developments, together with Freud's own personal predilections, led Freud to take the longing for the mother, for a return to the collective "ocean of divinity," in a literal way and to reduce the longing for the womb to a desire for sexual intercourse with the parents. Although Jung agrees with Freud that the attachment between children and parents has an erotic character, he does not agree that the aim of the erotic attachment is actual incest.[31] What is being sought, Jung maintains, is something for which Freud had only a negative appreciation: "The universal feeling of childhood innocence, the sense of security, of protection, of reciprocated love, of trust, of faith—a thing that has many names."[32] These, he thinks, are the essential contents of

31. Correctly speaking, in Jung's opinion, the term incest should be used only in the case of an adult who is psychologically incapable of linking his sexuality to its proper object. The same term applied to the problem of childhood development is misleading.
32. "Some Aspects of Modern Psychotherapy," volume 16, p. 32.

regressive tendencies; incest and other perverted sexual practices are by-products. Jung sees no reason to give the Oedipus
complex—which is an exclusively masculine affair—the status of
a prime cause; his own view is that the first attachment of both
the boy and the girl is to the mother, as an enfolding, protecting,
nourishment-giving being. These are the pleasures she provides;
they are at first nutritive and not sexual, and the one is not
reducible to or a substitute for the other.

Jung believes that, for the child, what Freud calls incest is
really a simple urge to remain a child and not let the libido flow
outward from the mother, or, later on, from both parents. The
natural development is that familiar objects in time lose their
compelling charm and the libido is forced to seek out new objects.[33] Especially at puberty, the child must consciously give up
his infantile wishes; otherwise the libido would stagnate and the
result would be impoverished development and "infantile" personality. But the task is not simple; it is not easy to overcome the
conservative adherence to an earlier and pleasant attitude. Nor
is it a simple matter to give up the former personality and abandon earlier objects of interest. Puberty rites and religion help the
individual make the transition, using the bridge of the symbol to
draw the libido away from infantile objects and desires toward
the representations of the parents and the past embodied in the
totem and the gods. These new "ancestors" and "parents" serve
to extend the family and provide the basis for communal identity
and social organization.

As for the origin of the symbols, Jung thinks that they were
not devised consciously but arose out of the unconscious by way

33. Only if the libido does not seek out new objects but gets "stuck," while the individual matures physically, do the Oedipus and Electra fantasies, which were previously
unconscious and inoperative, become conscious and active and, if not blocked and
resisted, lead to incest and murder. "This naturally does not happen with normal
people, nor in so-called 'amoral' primitive communities, otherwise the human race would
have perished long ago" (*The Theory of Psychoanalysis*, volume 4, p. 155).

of dreams, revelations, or intuition, and he finds evidence for this in the similarities between mythological and dream symbols. The implication is that in the course of evolution, appropriate symbols, instincts, and taboos arise which help mankind to control and understand its inner and outer environment. All the essential problems of survival and development were first faced and worked out in the unconscious; to a great extent, Jung would add, this is still true today.

At this juncture it is possible to undertake a description of the origin of human communities in sociological terms, as conceived by Jung. In a way, the world comes into being only when man discovers it, and he discovers it, both collectively and individually, only after "he sacrifices his containment in the primal mother, the original state of unconsciousness."[34] Hence the cosmic sacrifices and dismemberments that are a part of the creation myths and the similar but less grandiose rites that accompany puberty. Freud argues that what drives man to the discovery of the world, or, psychologically speaking, what forces the libido away from the mother and toward other objects, is the "incest barrier." Jung agrees, as long as the "mother" and the "incest barrier" are understood metaphorically, and "libido" is taken in a broader sense than the sexual. But, as we have seen, he does not agree that the incest taboo stems from the internalization of the murdered patriarch's prohibitions. Like other taboos, Jung simply attributes it to the peculiar evolutionary instinct of man. Indeed, he thinks that the incest barrier could not of itself have forced mankind out of his original psychic state of nondifferentiation. For the primary purpose of the incest taboo is not to prevent incest, but to forestall the social danger to the survival of the species originally embodied in matriarchal

34. *Symbols of Transformation,* volume 5, p. 417.

clans.[35] Jung draws heavily on the work of an English anthropologist, John Layard, who, in turn, is noticeably influenced by Jung's studies in mythology. Layard sketches a picture parallel to the one drawn by Freud of the original primal horde:

> Envisage man the animal, or, more important still, woman the animal, guarding her brood against all comers, jealous and murderous against any who should approach them, her mate providing the food and aiding in the defense....The brood grows up. Either the boys, after the "gang" stage, return and mate with her or with their sisters, or else they start other families with strange females who will be equally hostile in defense of theirs.[36]

No social life at all could come of this, Layard insists, and furthermore, no human beings ever lived like this, for no human beings ever lived without some kind of social life. For social life there must be cooperation as well as defense. The easiest form of cooperation would be within the family, but although inbreeding, Layard continues, is not necessarily biologically harmful, it is culturally harmful. It allows for no "new blood," that is, no new ideas or ways of doing things, in the family. The result would be a stereotyped and stagnant method of existence, which might lead to the family's and eventually to the species' extinction because of an inability to cope with and adapt to changing circumstances.

But if cultural interchange is essential to survival and progress, so is peace. New blood must be brought in so that experiences can be pooled, common needs dealt with, and the danger of the formation of smaller and smaller groups avoided;

35. In contrast to the Darwinian primal horde of the apes, on which Freud bases the original patriarchal life of mankind, Jung adheres to the anthropological studies of Jakob Bachofen *(Das Mutterrecht)*, Robert Briffault *(The Mothers)*, and others who argue that matriarchy was the first social form of human life.

36. John Layard, "The Incest Taboo and the Virgin Archetype," *Eranos-Jahrbuch*, Band 12 (1945), p. 269.

but the new blood must not be hostile. The solution is the first cousin marriage: the son marries the daughter of the mother's brother, and the daughter marries the son of the mother's brother.

Thus, the first cousin marriage is not a matter of avoiding incest, for which, Jung points out, there is plenty of opportunity under primitive conditions, but of the social necessity of spreading the family organization throughout the tribe for the sake of mutual obligations, cooperation, and defense. One could, therefore, define incest as "kinship libido," as an instinct that works to keep the family group intact. It is opposed by the "exogamous libido" that tends toward the separation from the immediate family and attachment to an outsider. On an archetypal level, the fear of the "devouring" mother, of personal extinction in the cosmic womb, and on a more physical level, the gradual loss of interest in familiar objects and the rising fascination with similar but as yet unknown objects are responsible for the activation of the "exogamous libido." Theoretically, this involves the interplay of opposites as the principle of all activity; where there is a drive toward endogamy, there must also be an opposed and compensating drive toward exogamy. Nevertheless, it would appear that at the beginning of human existence, both collective and individual, the endogamous tendency is stronger than the exogamous, or, what is more probable, the two tendencies are not yet fully differentiated.

The first cousin form of marriage is usually combined with the division of a group into two exogamous matrilineal moieties, strictly segregated in territory, customs, and tasks, but interdependent, so that the customs and tasks complement each other. Jung believes that the two moieties are the opposite sides of a unity[37] and concludes

37. The complementary interdependence of the two moieties is indicated by their typical names: Light and Dark, Sky and Earth, East and West, Male and Female, Right and Left.

that "the primary splitting of the psyche into conscious and unconscious seems to be the cause of the division within the tribe and the settlement. It is a division founded on fact but not consciously recognized as such."[38] In other words, mankind unconsciously externalized the two fundamentally opposed but related regions of the psyche into two opposed but related social groups. Like the projection of the psychic fears that gave rise to taboos, this externalization and the separation that went with it also served useful psychological and cultural functions: group self-awareness and identity were strengthened; a "safe" area for "exogamous interests" beyond the purely sexual was provided; and a suitable target for unconscious projections was created—in particular, the petty annoyances, fears, and hostilities could be displaced in a convenient way onto the "strangers" on the other side.

The two-part moiety, not unlike primitive biological organisms, in time split into four, so that eventually everyone married his or her first cousin on both the mother's and the father's side;[39] marriage became a group marriage and the population was divided into four marriage classes. Jung insists that the primitive marriage quaternion is not a conscious human invention, but something that existed long before consciousness; once established, men continued to follow the pattern simply because things were always done like that, that is, because of "tradition."

The combination of mutually related people concerned with each other's welfare, together with the introduction of new blood, both physically and spiritually, proved to be a powerful instrument for the survival and the development of culture. With an increase in population and an extension in consciousness, the

38. *Psychology of the Transference,* volume 16, p. 226.
39. For a more detailed explanation see John Layard, "The Incest Taboo and the Virgin Archetype," pp. 270–76.

exogamous tendency slowly expanded and thrust its endogamous counterpart into the background. The endogamous instinct, denied expression in the flesh, took up its psychological aspect, and found compensatory satisfaction in myths involving the incestuous union of gods, the similar prerogatives of kings, and so on. Later still, the exogamous order was extended to the point where nothing was left of the endogamous side except the incest taboo in the immediate family. The original social order sank into the unconscious and there gained strength, so that attempts were made through mythological and religious symbolism to reestablish consanguineous relations on a psychological level, and, through various religious communities and brotherhoods, national and political groupings, on a social level.[40]

Increasing secularization and internationalization have begun to abolish even these last remaining "barriers" and will probably continue to do so in the future. In the process, the libidinally related group is being replaced by an amorphous sea of isolated individuals whose artificial regrouping has given rise to the symptoms characteristic of the mass psyche. The "world" religions have, on the whole, turned out to be ineffective in extending the libidinal ties between men beyond national boundaries, while the modern organizing factor, the state, has turned out to be the most efficient machine for organizing and producing mass men. Thus, the social order, suffering from what could be called the disease of hyperexogamy, is approaching a condition of chaos. Where originally the community was regulated by mutual obligations and personal interrelationships, currently only force is capable of retaining a semblance of order. The exogamous tendency, once a positive

40. To paraphrase a Freudian concept, the process gave rise to "aim-inhibited endogamy."

stimulus for individual and cultural evolution, has now become destructive of the very things it helped to create.

On the other hand, the endogamous tendency, being an instinct, is not "satisfied by any mere substitute such as a creed, party, nation, or state. It wants the *human* connection."[41] It is inevitable, therefore, that under present conditions the endogamous instinct will make a renewed effort to intervene compensatorily and restore the consanguineous marriage. The recent attempts to establish communes and group marriages can be seen as one symptom of this compensation. But at this stage in human evolution, Jung maintains, the only meaningful compensation is the union of the divided components of the personality within the individual's own psyche. Such an integration is also the best remedy for the surrounding social chaos, and the only effective protection against the contagious influence of the mass psyche. But it is vitally important that this process of the union of opposites, of the endogamous marriage within the individual, takes place consciously. For the inner union does not occur on a personal level, in the ego, but in the Self, which is a synthesis of ego and transpersonal consciousness. If the consolidation occurs spontaneously or unconsciously, then, as was the case with Hitler, or as happens with the gurus and the messiahs of our own day, the Self is simply projected onto a leader. Under this new "totem," individuals then unite in an unconscious, souless herd, and easily succumb to group egoism, collective inflation, panic, and lust.

Thus, while the exogamous tendency led to the extension of cultural achievements from the family to ever larger and larger groups, in a parallel development the endogamous drive has led to the evolution of the spiritual realm from the totem, to the gods, and finally to the spirit within. Today, it presses for the

41. *Psychology of the Transference,* volume 16, p. 233.

"incestuous marriage" between ego-consciousness and the unconscious and the consequent birth of the Self.[42] The endogamous tendency "shows itself to be an instinctive force of a spiritual nature; and, regarded in this light, the life of the spirit on the highest level is a return to the beginnings, so that man's development becomes a recapitulation of the stages that lead ultimately to the perfection of life in the spirit."[43]

In the end, it is apparent that the disagreement between Jung and Freud on the nature of incest and its implications for cultural development is so fundamental as to be irreconcilable. Jung thinks that Freud's attempt to treat anthropological issues with theories based on individual psychology is nothing short of disastrous, and that the primal horde thesis, from which Freud derives all social beliefs and practices, is a myth with no foundation in either anthropological or psychic reality. Furthermore, if Freud finds Jung muddleheaded, Jung takes methodological exception to Freud's attempts to avoid multiplying explanations by reducing everything to one explanatory tenet, namely, the Oedipus complex, of which the primal horde is merely a sociological projection. It makes for a neat theory, with everything related to everything else; but in the process, Jung implies, the facts are distorted, and, if they do not happen to fit, glibly dismissed or ignored. Jung insists that it is illegitimate to apply to the psyche itself methods invented by the psyche to deal with objective "facts" and theories about those facts. He claims that psychology is in a unique position because it is the only science that has no reference points outside itself. All that can be done in psychology is to attempt a phenomenological description

42. For the man, the unconscious is normally represented by the figure of the anima (as his sister-mother) and in the woman by the figure of the animus (as her brother-father). Hence, the "incestuous marriage" in the union of the ego with the animus or anima.

43. *Psychology of the Transference*, volume 16, p. 229.

of the psyche's experience of inner and outer reality. Even then, the description is necessarily subjective; and since reality is multifaceted and interlocking, only several different approaches to the same problem can provide a more or less accurate, but never exhaustive, description.[44] Jung prefers to follow his data wherever they lead, even if sometimes they land him in what appears to be a blind alley or an apparent contradiction.

GROUP PSYCHOLOGY

There is no area where there seems to be so much agreement between Jung and Freud as in matters relating to group psychology. Both accept Gustave Le Bon's classic description of the crowd and agree that when in a crowd the individual reverts to a primitive and emotional intellectual state. Both assume that group psychology was the original form of human consciousness and assert that under conditions of stress or intense emotional involvement that form of consciousness again comes to the fore. Contact with this primeval level of the psyche taps or constellates normally dormant energies and releases the psyche from culturally and consciously imposed standards and restrictions. In the process, the group becomes highly emotional and suggestible, while its sense of reality and reason are eclipsed.

The formation of a group automatically gives rise to the need for a leader. It then attaches itself to the leader in a blindly passionate way and expects strong authority and firm rule. In Western man,[45] Jung writes, "we have to reckon with a patriar-

44. The same difficulty sometimes arises in studies of the objective, physical world as well. For example, both wave and particle theory are able to account for the behavior of light, but we may never know which is the more "correct" explanation, or whether each explains a valid aspect which is, however, incompatible with the other.
45. Freud would simply say all men.

chal or hierarchical orientation of the psyche which causes it instinctively to seek and cling to this order."[46] In part, this has to do with the residue of the paternal imago of childhood, but a more important influence is the unconscious heritage of the race. And Freud would again agree—and universalize Jung's contention—that the loss of firm authority leads to "intellectual, political, and social anarchy which is repugnant to the soul of European man, accustomed as he is to a patriarchal order."[47]

In all this the two men concur. Their explanations for the cohesion of the group and the nature of its attachment to the leader, however, are somewhat different. Freud ascribes the cohesion and the attachment to a two-way sexually inhibited libidinal tie between the individual and the leader, who is internalized as the ego-ideal, and between the individual and others who share the same ego-ideal. The perception of the common, shared quality is responsible for the libidinal, really narcissistic, bonds among the members of the group. The mysterious power or mana that distinguishes the leader and accounts for his hold over the group Freud attributes to a projection of unconscious, ambivalent feelings toward authority figures; the feelings derive from the collective memory of the patriarch of the primal horde and from the individual memory of childhood experiences of one's own father. These primeval and childhood memories, the two-way erotic relationship, and the regression to group consciousness together explain the contagious and suggestion-prone temper of a group.

Jung would demur in part and then extend the argument. The libidinal, narcissistic tie does not have to be a product of sexually inhibited libido; even in Freud's terms, narcissism is not the result of aim-inhibited and sublimated libido. And the archaic

46. "Psychotherapy Today," volume 16, p. 99.
47. *Ibid.*, p. 103.

and childhood memories of awe-inspiring authority are not limited to a father figure but include such figures as mothers, uncles, shamans, chiefs, kings, priests, and only later, and primarily in the West, fathers. Any one of these, therefore, can become a group leader and evoke the mana-producing projection. Jung also leaves room for the possibility of the existence of a mana-personality impressive in its own right and not because of projection. As for the regression to group psychology, Jung adds several intermediate levels—family, clan, tribe, nation, race—before speaking of the collective psyche of the species, where Freud locates the memories of the primal horde. This gradation does not, however, imply that the deeper the regression, the more intense the sense of unity. The intensity and nature of the unity of the group depends on the types of archetypes or collective images and emotions activated. Moreover, in the unconscious the gradations are hardly regimented or even ordered; a better image would be that of a goulash in which all the elements and flavors are combined, with the difference that under appropriate conditions, one of the elements can return to its original state and even increase its energy and size at the expense of the others.

Jung would probably argue that a spontaneously unified group can be formed in two ways: first, an intense emotion, or an emotional situation to which a number of people are subjected, can cause a temporary lapse of ego consciousness, a "loss of soul," and a regression to the collective psyche; second, identical archetypes may be energized in the unconscious of a number of people because of certain objective conditions, conscious attitudes, or evolutionary processes, and suddenly burst upon consciousness, giving rise to spontaneous groupings with emotional ties and uniform behavior.

Spontaneous groups sometimes turn into organized

associations; and if an organization, whether religious, military, social, economic, or political, is to maintain unity and similarities among the members of attitudes and responses, an identical psychic experience must be shared by all the members. But in organized groups, the identical experience has to be induced deliberately and artificially, often through education and propaganda; these, in turn, make use of symbols, myths, or ideas that evoke the unifying emotional commitment. The more the symbols reflect the psychic heritage and condition of the members of the group, the more effective they are as a consolidating force. They provide the inner and outer objects in which the psyche encounters or projects its unity with transpersonal contents. Thus, Freud was not wrong, in Jung's view, about the essential mechanism of group formation, but in this, as in other matters, he saw it too narrowly and from a strictly sexual point of view.

Both Freud and Jung also comment on the sense of omnipotence and freedom from moral restriction that leaders and members of a group often feel. Freud defines this phenomenon as a *mania,* produced by the fusion of the ego and the superego. Normally there exists a tension between the narcissistic desires of the ego and the idealistic and prohibitive demands of the superego. If for some reason the two agencies fuse, either in an individual or in a group, and if to this fusion is added the reversion to the primitive group mind, then the person or the group "in a mood of triumph and self-satisfaction, disturbed by no self-criticism" can enjoy the abolition of all inhibitions, self-reproaches, and feelings of consideration for others.[48] Furthermore, the leader, like the patriarch of the primal horde, is usually a man who tends to be egoistic and have few aim-inhibited ties, so that the cleavage between his ego and his

48. Freud, *Standard Edition,* volume 18, p. 132.

superego is very slight or nonexistent. And where a split does exist, as soon as he becomes the ego-ideal of others, fusion occurs; the leader then feels a tremendous sense of mastery, self-confidence, autonomy, and omnipotence. Like the absolutely narcissistic primal father, Freud writes, he is the "Superman" of whom Nietzsche spoke, although *megalomania* would be the more clinical designation.

Jung, on the other hand, argues that such exuberant, egoistic, and "God-Almighty" feelings are the outcome of individual or group identification with the transpersonal contents of the collective unconscious.[49] But the two men essentially agree on the general process responsible for such feelings. They differ in terminology and in the basic assumptions underlying their concepts. Freud speaks of "mania" and the fusion of the ego with the largely unconscious superego; Jung speaks of "psychic inflation" and the identification of the ego with contents of the collective unconscious. Both believe that the leader's power and stature derive, to a great extent, from the followers' projections, which are conditioned by the inherited memory of the species—the memory of the primal horde for Freud, the archetypes for Jung—and by the particular experience of the individual.

Given the results of their investigations of the unconscious and of its influence on group psychology, both Jung and Freud are wary of mass movements and mass psychology. Their attitude is an antidote to the overly benevolent view of human nature posited by the Enlightenment and inherited by the twentieth century as a blind faith in the "masses," or in the "people." Jung, however, is less pessimistic in this regard than Freud, who has an essentially negative and derogatory opinion of the unconscious; since men in a crowd sink to the level of the un-

49. See chapter 2 of this book for a detailed explication.

conscious, he has an equally dour view of the "masses" and mass psychology. Furthermore, Freud believes that the mass of mankind, because of the heritage of the primal horde, is content only under firm patriarchal rule and hence is a thoroughgoing elitist. In his essay "Why War?" (1933), Freud proposes "to educate an upper stratum of men with independent minds," who have subordinated their instincts to "the dictatorship of reason" and "whose business it would be to give direction to the dependent masses."[50]

On the other hand, Jung is no great exponent of egalitarianism and radical democracy, and he, too, harbors many aristocratic attitudes about the masses and about the human species in general. However, Jung's appraisal of the unconscious is much more positive than Freud's. Although cognizant of the primitive, irrational, and destructive elements of the unconscious, he nevertheless maintains that the unconscious is also the source of all psychic life and creativity. Consequently, for Jung, masses and mass movements are not always to be despised and controlled. For most new psychic developments and cultural attitudes appear first on the lowest social levels where the unconscious holds sway, relatively unhindered by rational considerations. A dictatorship of reason, whether psychological or political, would only repress the nonrational, emotional components of the psyche, distort them further, and link them to the more primitive and inhuman drives of the unconscious. Strict rational rule of the masses, even if it were possible, can only produce mass psychoses and periodic orgies of collective rebellion, brutality, and violence—the very things it is meant to prevent—and would stifle creativity as well.

50. Freud, *Standard Edition*, volume 22, p. 212. Freud also states, in the same place, that "one instance of the innate and ineradicable inequality of men is their tendency to fall into two classes of leaders and followers. The latter constitute the vast majority; they stand in need of an authority which will make decisions for them and to which they for the most part offer an unqualified submission."

GROUP PSYCHOLOGY AND FASCISM

To Jung's contention that the Germans suffered from collective hysteria, psychopathic inferiority, and psychic inflation in which the Wotan archetype played a vital role, the Freudian studies of the Nazi phenomenon add the element of an authoritarian personality structure in the middle class in general, and in the German middle class in particular. Indeed, this notion has become the most popular psychological explanation for the tragic events that transpired in Germany under Hitler.

Wilhelm Reich, in *The Mass Psychology of Fascism* (1933), was the first to assert that the psychological foundation of Nazism was the ambiguous attitude of the German lower middle class toward authority.[51] The ambiguity consisted in a desire for strict authority, indeed a respect and love for it, together with a repressed rebellion against authority and a fear and hatred of it. This ambiguous attitude was translated into a behavior pattern characterized by servile obedience of superiors and authoritarian oppression of inferiors. Hence the support of Hitler's rebellion against the established order, together with the unquestioning respect for and submission to the Führer, and the imposition of an authoritarian hierarchy throughout the society. Authoritarianism of this type feeds upon itself; it forms a vicious circle aptly depicted by the Germans themselves as "the bicycle personality": to maintain balance and motion it needs constantly to bow to those above and kick those below. In this manner it satisfies the desire for an identification with authority and for subservience to it and disposes of the repressed hostility and aggression generated by the fear of authority and the submission to it.

---

51. Reich was a restless, imaginative genius who eventually went insane. He is an embarrassment to many adherents of Freud, who, nevertheless, make use of his ideas, frequently without mentioning their source.

Reich argues that such a personality structure is developed in the patriarchal middle-class family through the father's repression of the sexual instincts in the name of morality. Since, for Reich, all libido is sexual energy defined in a genital way, the repression of genital sexuality lies at the root of various mental and physical pathologies. The most common manifestation of such sexual repression is the development of a character structure that makes men feel weak and impotent, that makes them afraid, fearful of authority, obedient, shy, docile, and "good." But these are in fact the socioeconomic requirements of the lower middle class in a patriarchal bourgeois society; the strictures of morality and the institution of the family through which these strictures are imposed upon the children are merely the instruments through which such a society achieves its aims and ensures its survival.

Reich's basic thesis was adopted and given a historical background by Erich Fromm in *Escape from Freedom* (1942) and then found its way into *The Authoritarian Personality* (1950), edited by Theodor Adorno and others. This study, which purports to tie the authoritarian personality to an entire complex of fascist and anti-Semitic traits, was the major collaborative effort of the Institute for Social Research, first at Frankfurt am Main and then at Columbia University, whose faculty included Theodor Adorno, Erich Fromm, Max Horkheimer, Herbert Marcuse, and Franz Neumann.[52]

Wilhelm Reich's analysis of the Nazi movement is the ap-

52. Marcuse especially has taken up Reich's initial attempt during the early thirties to unite Marx and Freud and to turn the pessimistic, conservative Freudian social theories into a new, utopian, revolutionary political philosophy. In a manner analogous to Marx's reinterpretation of Hegel, Marcuse accepts the basic Freudian categories but argues that they are really overlaid by the historical and cultural experience of the time; once they are dereified, that is, understood in their historical context, and their ideological veneer is removed, the essential concepts turn out to be valid critical insights into the repressive nature of the human condition under capitalism and thus allow for the possibility of future liberation.

plication of Freud's general theories on group psychology, as contained in *Group Psychology and Analysis of the Ego* (1921), to a specific case. It was Freud who argued that, because of the primal horde experience, men are both passionately intolerant of and obedient to authority; they want to identify with it while remaining subservient to it; they want both to love and to fear their rulers; they desire to be oppressed, to be ruled with force, strength, and violence; and they interpret any sign of kindness on the part of their leaders as weakness. It was also Freud who maintained that the species' primal horde experience, which is responsible for such attitudes toward authority, is recapitulated in every family in the child's relationship to the father. In both cases, it is the father who initially restricts the free expression of genital sexuality.

Thus, Reich, Fromm, Adorno and others took what Freud considered to be universally applicable principles, reduced them to characteristic features of the German lower middle class or of the middle class in general, and then argued that therein was the explanation of Nazism. Once this was done, it was but a short step to the equation of the authoritarian personality with fascism and anti-Semitism, and then, in turn, to the suspicion of fascism and anti-Semitism in every capitalist middle class in the Western world. The authoritarian personality, with Freud a universal characteristic, was particularized in the German middle class and then was universalized again as the fascist personality.

This reduction of fascism to the authoritarian personality was the result of a facile application of Freud's basic theories on group psychology rather than the outcome of a direct examination of the psychological forces actually involved. Such muddled, reductionist theorizing as this could have been avoided had it been pointed out that Freud's views on authority and group psychology were themselves strongly influenced by his own cultural milieu. They were, therefore, indeed applicable to Germany and could be used as at least a partial explanation of the Nazi phenomenon. They were not, however, universally applicable. In an indirect way, this argument was eventually made by Herbert Marcuse in *Eros and Civilization* (1950), but it was never proposed by the Freudians who were concerned with explaining German fascism.

For his part, Jung was well aware of the mass psychology that contributed to the rise of fascism, and he too mentioned the authoritarian tradition of the German state and culture. But unlike the Freudians, he did not regard the authoritarian character structure as the basic psychological underpinning of the Nazi movement. It had its place, but it was merely one of a series of psychological characteristics that converged to produce the political deviation of the time, as we have seen in chapter six of this book.

SUPEREGO AND CONSCIENCE

As with everything else, Freud traces the origins of the superego to the murder of the primal father and to its individual recapitulation in the Oedipus complex. Because of these initial unsuccessful attempts to achieve uninhibited instinctual satisfaction, the two instincts, eros and aggression, are repressed and then sublimated into affection and fear. The authority and prohibitions of the father are internalized and confront the ego as the superego. It should be pointed out that in the primal horde the internalization occurs because of the remorse and desire for identification with the father that arise after the successful patricide and incest, while in the individual it is a product of thwarted instinctual satisfaction after an unsuccessful attempt to repeat the patricide and incest of the primal horde. Still, Freud maintains that the internalization of the parental prohibitions and identification with the father are the same in both cases. The tension between the ego and the superego is felt as the sense of guilt. The aggressive instinct supplies the energy for self-punishment, while the sex instinct provides the energy for neurotic symptoms. In its final version, therefore, Freud's concept of the superego is made up of three agencies and four functions: conscience (self-observation), ego-ideal (aspiration), and superego (condemnation and punishment). In each individual, the superego created by the Oedipus complex links up with the phylogenic acquisition, or the "archaic heritage," of mankind. Unconscious memories of the primal horde, the patricide, the resulting guilt, and the taboos against murder and incest are an influential part of this inheritance. But in the course of time, other acquisitions are added to the common heritage. The progressive repression and displacement of instinctual drives and the internalization of environmental and cultural experience give rise to new psychic dispositions. These dispositions are present in the newborn child and serve as an indispensible aid to his cultural adaptation. For example, Freud notes in his *Three Essays on the Theory of Sexuality* (1905) that the various sexual inhibitions—disgust, feelings of shame, aesthetic and moral ideals—seem to be a product of education, "but in reality [their] development is organically determined and fixed by heredity, and it can occasionally occur without any help at all from education."[53] Similarly, in "Thoughts for the Times on War and Death," Freud observes: "Every internal compulsion which has been of service in the development of human beings was originally . . . nothing but an external one. Those who are born today bring with them as an inherited constitution some degree

53. Freud, *Standard Edition*, volume 7, pp. 177–78.

of a tendency (disposition) towards transmutation of egoistic into social instincts, and this disposition is easily stimulated to achieve that effect."[54] And oddly enough, despite all his insistence that it is impossible to "get rid of man's aggressive inclinations," Freud nevertheless thinks that some people, himself included, find violence and war abhorrent, not because of moral or rational considerations, but for organic reasons. He thinks that the cultural process, which gradually displaces and restricts the original instinctual aims, eventually modifies the basic instincts to the point where the "sensations which were pleasurable to our ancestors have become indifferent or even intollerable to ourselves."[55] Thus, the superego turns out to be the primary instrument for the modification of the psyche, and the vehicle, both cultural and organic, for the transmission of the collective traditions and values of one generation to the next.

Jung does not think much of the entire business. The only proposition he agrees with is that it is the father who stands for the world of moral commandments and prohibitions. Jung, however, means this in a quite different way from Freud, for he maintains that "for lack of information about conditions in prehistoric times, it remains an open question how far the first moral laws arose from dire necessity rather than from the family preoccupations of the tribal father."[56] Nonetheless, Jung sees the father as the representative of the "spirit," whose function it is to oppose pure instinctuality, and claims that this role is projected onto him regardless of his personal qualities. "As for Freud's concept of the 'superego,' " Jung writes, "it is a furtive attempt to smuggle the time-honoured image of Jehovah in the dress of

54. Freud, *Standard Edition*, volume 14, p. 282. I quote from a better translation by E. Colburn Mayne in *Sigmund Freud: Character and Culture*, ed. Philip Reiff (New York: Collier Books, 1963), p. 115.

55. Freud, *Standard Edition*, volume 22, p. 214.

56. *Symbols of Transformation*, volume 5, p. 260.

psychological theory. For my part, I prefer to call things by the names under which they have always been known," in this case, conscience.[57] From Jung's point of view, then, the Freudian superego is an expression of the patriarchal Judeo-Christian tradition that has provided the collective moral code of Western man. It undeniably exists and exerts an unconscious or semiconscious influence on motivations and behavior, but by calling the function by its historical name, Jung wants to emphasize the fact that individual conscience and the collective ethical code do not always coincide.

To begin with, Jung provides his own description of the origin and the evolution of conscience. He traces its source to the primordial images, to those "collective representations" that govern the psychic and social life of primitive men, in much the same way as our lives are governed and molded by generally accepted beliefs and values: they intervene automatically in every decision and choice and influence the formation of concepts. The first "moral reaction" is actually a sort of shock that occurs when the psyche is confronted with a deviation on the part of oneself or another from the habitual ways of viewing and doing things. The primitive mind, especially, fears anything unusual or different and considers it "immoral," that is, not in accordance with the customary *mores*. In modern man, this reaction is usually less acute and is felt more as a sense of discomfort or a "twinge of conscience"; nevertheless, it still reflects the original shock experience of the psyche. Moral laws are a late codification of the generally accepted "ideal" modes of behavior. Consequently, they appear identical with inner moral attitudes and reactions with conscience. But this identity does not always exist in fact. It sometimes happens that a conflict arises between the moral code and the demands of conscience. In

57. "Freud and Jung: Contrasts," volume 4, p. 339.

most instances, the conflict is resolved by adhering to the moral code and suppressing or ignoring the proddings of conscience; without the support of the collective moral code, personal conscience easily succumbs to weakness. An individual requires unusual courage and unshakable faith in the rightness of his conscience to follow its dictates, when these conflict with established ways.

The interesting problem, however, is how the conscience acquires the conviction and sense of justification to rise, at times, above the moral code and refuse to submit to its dictates. History shows that the individual who takes such a stand is always, and according to the moral precepts of the time, justly condemned as a criminal. Nevertheless, since ancient days men have referred to conscience as the "voice of God," although they have also insisted that there is a "true" and a "false" conscience; apparently the gods may lead one astray, or, according to a later explanation, the voice of conscience may really be the voice of an evil spirit.

Jung approaches these matters from a psychological perspective. He defines conscience as an autonomous psychic content that asserts itself in spite of and often contrary to an individual's personal intentions. Like every other autonomous psychic factor or complex, conscience cannot be the product of learning or education, and the belief that it is the *vox dei* attests to its transpersonal autonomy and its numinous character; for like all archetypal ideas, it partakes of the manifestation of mana and possesses a powerful dynamism that has a profound effect on human behavior. Like all archetypes, this one is bipolar, which is why conscience is seen as morally ambivalent: like the Yahwistic God-image it is "both just and unjust, kindly and cruel, truthful and deceitful."[58] In the Christian version of

58. "A Psychological View of Conscience," volume 10, p. 448.

God as the *Summum Bonum*, the negative aspects are simply assigned to God's adversary, Satan. Only in the human acts of cognition and deliberation does the archetype of conscience acquire a moral quality.

Having translated the various phenomena associated with conscience into psychological concepts, Jung still has not answered the question of justification. What exactly takes place in a conflict between a moral precept and the voice of conscience, or, similarly, in the case of two conflicting moral laws or duties? Here, if conscience or one of the alternatives is not simply suppressed, a creative act must occur in order to produce the final judgment. Such a creative act, like all creative developments, springs from two sources, according to Jung: the rational consciousness and the nonrational unconscious; and it entails a discursive cooperation between these two agencies of the psyche. Jung calls this active connection between the two psychic realms the "transcendent function." A more familiar Jungian term for it is the Self, for the function can develop into a distinct psychic entity, encompassing and transcending the individual's conscious ego. This is the personality that stands behind the daring "act of conscience."

Jung argues that if it were true that there is nothing behind man's decisions of conscience but collective standards on the one hand and the natural instincts on the other, then every breach of morality would simply be a rebellion of instinct—as indeed it is in Freud. "In that case valuable and meaningful innovations would be impossible, for the instincts are the oldest and most conservative element in man and beast alike. Such a view," he concludes, "forgets the creative instinct which, although it can behave like an instinct, is seldom found in nature and is confined almost exclusively to *Homo sapiens.*"[59] There is no

59. *Transformation Symbolism in the Mass,* volume 11, p. 258 fn.

creativity where there is blind adherence to custom and the suppression of conflicts and new impulses; only the patient endurance of conflicts of conscience allows the archetype to constellate and create a solution possessing "that compelling authority not unjustly characterized as the voice of God."[60] The nature of the solution then embraces both the conscious perception and the unconscious insights and gives expression to the deepest foundations of the personality, which transcend the purely personal ego.[61]

ARCHAIC HERITAGE AND THE ARCHETYPES

Jung is highly critical of the concept of an "archaic heritage" that constitutes an essential part of the Freudian superego. Since Freud rejects the archetypes—the hypothesis of the existence of a priori, instinctive modes of apprehension and behavior—as mystical and unscientific, his superego, Jung argues, can only be a sort of Weltanschauung, composed of consciously acquired traditions and values, some of which have been repressed and become unconscious. It is these unconscious elements that Freud calls the "archaic heritage," and which are, according to him, inherited; but this is impossible, for it would imply the possibility of the inheritance of "acquired ideas," and there is no scientific evidence for this. Yet Freud's concept of the superego, and to a great extent his theories on group psychology and cultural evolution, does rely heavily on the possibility, indeed the necessity, of the inheritance of dispositions and attitudes. Jung

60. "A Psychological View of Conscience," volume 10, p. 455.
61. On the basis of this exposition, Jung proposes that a distinction be made between the moral and the ethical aspects of conscience. Morality, stemming as it does from the *mores*, is the observance of customary modes of behavior. Ethics, derived from *ethos*, is a commitment based on the creative acts of conscience of the spirit or the Self.

maintains that Freud was forced to believe in this possibility because his practical experience taught him that there are many cases where the act of conscience takes place unconsciously. "It is therefore probable," Jung concludes, "that the 'archaic vestiges' in the superego are a concession to the archetypes theory and imply a fundamental doubt as to the absolute dependence of unconscious contents on consciousness."[62]

In truth, the argument here against Freud is much stronger than Jung makes it. Freud never concealed the fact that he was an adherent of the Lamarckian theory of evolution through the inheritance of "acquired characteristics." In his biography of Freud, Ernest Jones discusses his uncompromising stand, even in the face of the scientific evidence against the theory.[63] Jones cites Freud's earliest use of the thesis in 1893, long before Jung proposed the theory of the archetypes. And as Freud's interest turned to sociological issues in his later years, he came to rely on it more and more. Thus, in his last book, *Moses and Monotheism* (1939), he deliberately undertakes a fairly long discussion of the problems associated with the question of "archaic heritage." In the course of the discussion, he clearly asserts that "the archaic heritage of human beings comprises not only dispositions but also subject-matter—memory-traces of the experience of earlier generations."[64] He makes this assertion, he says, fully aware of the fact that his position is made "difficult by the present attitude of biological science, which refuses to hear of the inheritance of acquired characters by succeeding generations. I must, however," he continues, "in all modesty confess that nevertheless I cannot do without this factor in

62. "A Psychological View of Conscience," volume 10, p. 440.
63. Apparently Freud planned to write a book with one of his followers, Sandor Ferenczi, on the relation of Lamarckism to psychoanalysis and prepared an outline, which, unfortunately, has been lost.
64. Freud, *Standard Edition*, volume 23, p. 99.

biological evolution.''[65] This is the only way in which Freud can bridge the gulf between individual and group psychology and account for psychological and cultural development. He maintains that in man the "archaic heritage" corresponds to the inborn instincts in animals by which the experiences of the species are passed on to succeeding generations.

It appears, therefore, that rather than accept the "mysticism" of the archetypes, Freud prefers to remain with the "superstition" of acquired characteristics. Jung, of course, also had to deal with these problems, for with the discovery of the unconscious and the rejection of the tabula rasa conception of the psyche, the psychoanalytic theorists had somehow to account for psychic inheritance and evolution. Although no one except religious fundamentalists any longer disputes the evolutionary development of man's physiology and anatomy, when it comes to the psyche there are still many who prefer to believe it must have sprung fully armed, like Pallas Athene, from the head of Zeus. Freud, disposed to place psychic evolution on an organic foundation, was forced to adopt Lamarckism; Jung was not so restricted and proposed a psychological hypothesis to deal with the same problem—he postulated the existence and inheritance of the archetypes.

Since Jung's theory of the archetypes is so difficult, it is necessary to summarize it here in order to bring into focus the differences between Jung and Freud on this issue. Jung defines an archetype as a latent structural disposition that expresses the dynamic contents and processes of the collective unconscious in primordial images; like the basic biological functions, most important primordial images are probably common to all ages and all races. An archetype can be conceived of as a mnemonic deposit, an imprint, or an engram, which has developed through

65. *Ibid.*, p. 100.

the condensation of countless, ever-recurring, psychic experiences. Thus, "if one holds the view that a particular anatomical structure is a product of environmental conditions working on living matter, then the primordial image, in its constant and universal distribution, would be the product of equally constant and universal influences from without."[66] And once formed, like the organic structure, it acts according to natural law and continually reawakens certain experiences or formulates them in an appropriate way. One could relate the archaic mythological motifs, which form the primordial images, to natural forms, but that would not explain why the natural objects and events do not appear in the psyche in their natural, undisguised form. Jung argues that to the environmental experience must be added the given structure of the brain, which apparently "does not owe its peculiar nature merely to the influence of surrounding conditions, but also and just as much to the peculiar and autonomous quality of living matter, i.e., to a law inherent in life itself."[67] Thus the primordial image is a product of and is related to both continually recurring natural processes and events, and inner determinants of psychic life and life in general. Because of its dual nature it is well suited to coordinate and give meaning to both outer and inner perceptions and guide action along paths corresponding to this meaning. It frees psychic energy from the enormous confusion that would result from sheer perception by leading the mind back to nature and canalizing pure instincts into mental forms. In this it is the necessary counterpart of instinct, but it is also the mechanism without which the apprehension of a new situation would be impossible.

The primordial image is also the precursor of the idea, or, to put it in a slightly different way, the idea is an abstracted, col-

---

66. *Psychological Types,* volume 6, p. 444.
67. *Ibid.*

lective version of the primordial image with the visual qualities lacking. Jung distinguishes between secondary ideas, or thoughts, and primary ideas. Secondary ideas are derivations from primary ideas and mere products of thought processes. Primary ideas, on the other hand, carry the formulated meaning of a primordial image, and like that image, exist a priori as the given possibilities of thought-combinations.[68] Because such ideas are abstracted from the primordial images, some philosophers ascribe a transcendental quality to them; however Jung holds that this does not really belong to the ideas, but to the under-lying archetype.

SUBLIMATION AND INSTINCTS

Jung also takes Freud to task over the notion of "sublimation." Sublimation, he states, is the alchemical trick of turning the base into the noble, the bad into the good, the useless into the useful. But unfortunately, he continues, "the secret of converting energy without the consumption of a still greater quantity of energy has never yet been discovered by the physicists. Sublimation remains, for the present, a pious wish-fulfillment invented for silencing inopportune questions."[69] In other words, Freud invented, or rather borrowed, the alchemical idea because of the necessity of somehow dealing with such evils as incest, patricide, and other drives incompatible with culture. But Jung maintains that, in fact, sublimation is simply a more subtle form of repression; for how sublimation "is to be done without creating a new repression nobody can quite explain."[70] Moreover, the ego certainly cannot sublimate at will, nor will

68. *Ibid.*, p. 437.
69. "Sigmund Freud in his Historical Setting," volume 15, p. 37.
70. "Psychotherapy and a Philosophy of Life," volume 16, p. 77.

what it is not given as a potentiality. Only inexorable need and absolute necessity can effectively inhibit an instinct, and even then, only for a time. In spite of his objections, therefore, Jung does not reject the concept, but he does want to redefine it and delineate its mode of operation. For him, sublimation is not the "transmutation" of instincts, but the spontaneous "transfer" of energy from one instinctual form to another, from a physical instinct, for example, to its corresponding archetypal form. Such a transfer, however, is never permanent, and if willfully sustained, is dangerous to the well-being of the individual.

Unlike Freud, Jung does not limit the instincts to organic, egoistic eros and aggression and then have to worry about how to alter their nature and distribute their energy to various areas of social and cultural life. Jung defines instinct as any *"impulsion toward certain activities"* including "all psychic processes whose energies are not under conscious control."[71] The stimulus for the impulsion can be either an inner or an outer one, and the mechanism of instinct can also be triggered either psychically or organically. Psychic processes that are usually functions of the will can become instinctive if supplied with unconscious energy; this occurs if they are repressed, or if conscious control is lost because of fatigue, intoxication, or other morbid cerebral conditions. If such processes become *automatized,* Jung relegates them to the automatic processes, for they no longer possess the impulsion of instincts.

Among the numerous human instincts, Jung includes a social instinct. For him, "man is also a social being and not just a bundle of egoistic instinct. . . . He carries his social imperatives within himself, *a priori,* as an inborn necessity."[72] The same is true of mankind's religious, artistic, and ethical functions. Thus,

71. *Psychological Types,* volume 6, p. 451.
72. "Some Crucial Points in Psychoanalysis," volume 4, p. 278.

Jung is spared the necessity of claiming that all cultural and religious feelings are nothing but repressed sexual drives that are sublimated into higher forms of expression. This would be like saying, Jung declares, that electricity is "nothing but" a water-fall piped into a turbine, and that electricity is, therefore, actually a "culturally deformed" waterfall.[73]

For Jung, the instincts are not just biological phenomena, but are at the same time meaningful fantasy structures with a symbolic character. Every instinct is linked a priori with a corresponding psychic image or "viewpoint" of a situation. This, Jung argues, can be proved indirectly in cases of the symbiosis of plants and animals, while in man it is possible to have a direct "insight into that remarkable world of 'magical' ideas which cluster round the instincts and not only express their form and mode of manifestation but 'trigger them off.'"[74] On the primitive level, instinct reveals itself as a complex interplay of physiology, rites, taboos, class-systems, and tribal lore that "impose a restrictive form on the instinct from the beginning, preconsciously, and make it serve a higher purpose."[75]

Finally, Jung takes exception to the opposition that Freud sets up between his two primary instincts. "Logically," Jung agrees, "the opposite of love is hate, and of Eros, Phobos (fear); but psychologically it is the will to power."[76] Where there is love, there is no will to power, and where there is a will to power, there love is lacking. These are the two opposites, and the man who adopts the standpoint of the one inevitably bears the other as his compensatory shadow. So it is not a question of avoiding one by emphasizing the other—they are inseparable. Only an awareness of this fact and a willingness consciously to endure the tension

73. "The Role of the Unconscious," volume 10, p. 8.
74. *Mysterium Coniunctionis*, volume 14, pp. 417–18.
75. *Ibid.*, p. 418.
76. *Two Essays*, volume 7, p. 52.

between them can save an individual from the perversions and neuroses that arise if one of the sides is repressed. Like Freud, therefore, Jung assumes an essential polarity in the psyche. But he thinks that Freud's basic polarity is first of all wrong and second, too limited. For Jung every instinct, every archetype, and the psyche as a whole are composed of opposing and complementary principles; out of the tension between them comes the physical and psychological energy of life.

Jung thinks that Freud's own peculiar psychological bias led him to formulate the primary opposition in the way he did. Eros is not the same as life, but since Freud reduced all life to Eros, then naturally the opposite of life is death. Moreover, "we all feel that the opposite of our own highest principle must be purely destructive, deadly, and evil. We refuse to endow it with any positive life-force; hence we avoid and fear it."[77] Western religions and ideologies are the best examples of this attitude, and it seems to have also infested Freud's thinking.

The differences between Jung and Freud on this issue have important implications for their attitudes about politics. Since for Freud, the will to power is a manifestation of the death instinct with its destructiveness and violence, then obviously the leading principle of politics is by definition dangerous and antagonistic to all culture and life. For Jung, the will to power may be tied to the aggressive instinct, but it is not necessarily linked to the death instinct. Moreover, in Jung's view, the death instinct with its regressive and incestuous urges on the one hand, and its desire for rebirth and immortality on the other, is not primarily characterized by destruction and violence. The pursuit of political power, therefore, is not inherently inimical or antithetical to humanistic and creative impulses.

77. *Ibid.*, p. 53.

10

Some Thoughts about Democracy

Jung does not espouse liberal democracy as a generally applicable, ideal form of government. Rather, he holds an organic view of the relationship between the individual, the society, and the state, so that, where there is no historical, social, and political basis for a democratic order, it is unwise to graft it on by decree. Moreover, given his opinion of the pernicious influence of sheer numbers, Jung would certainly argue that democracy is possible only on a small scale.

Furthermore, Jung is skeptical of the belief in ongoing human development and progress. He acknowledges changes, the rise of new archetypal dominants, the emergence of new psychic and social conflicts, and the appearance of new integrating symbols and styles of life. But he also sees that in the end every culture and civilization fades and dies, and there is no assurance that a new culture will develop, or that it will be superior to those that went before. Usually periods of cultural advance are followed by declines, and even returns to barbarism, and if there is any development of the kind we call "progress," it is probably of a slow, spiraling kind.

The argument that follows, then, is my own and not Jung's, although it is grounded in his conception of human nature; it would be presumptuous to claim that Jung would agree with all of it. But I would argue that Jung's conception of conscience, which affirms the ability of the individual to achieve an autonomous and yet not egoistic resolution of the major conflicts in his personal and social life, implies that for a group of such individuals democracy is the social and political order that best conforms to their essential nature. This conclusion is not the result of speculation or abstract theory but is based on an appraisal of the present psychic potential of the individual and supported by the history of the psychomoral development of mankind.

The group ethic, based on taboos and customs, with clan or tribal responsibility for upholding that ethic, was the first stage in man's moral evolution.[1] The rise of male-dominated societies marked the second stage. Here the individual was initiated into obligations and modes of behavior decreed by an ancestor deity, a collective projection of the masculine spirit or Self. Then came the Heroes, the mana-personalities, the founders of religions, who either provided models for imitation or promulgated moral rules in the name of the tribal god. Next came the kings and priests who, as representatives and spokesmen for the gods, assumed or, in many cases, were saddled with the responsibility for the moral life and well-being of the community.

Through each of these stages, individual consciousness became more differentiated and separated from the group, until the individual himself accepted the responsibility for his own moral behavior. He voluntarily identified with the traditional

1. Erich Neumann, in his *Depth Psychology and a New Ethic* (New York: G. P. Putnam's Sons, 1969), outlines the practical implications of Jung's notion of conscience. He, too, speaks of the stages of ethical development, but his treatment is somewhat different from mine.

values of the community and tried to guide his consciousness and his demeanor in accordance with the moral laws. Since his instincts and his unconscious did not always share his conscious ideals, he had to learn to suppress or repress incompatible drives. Morality at this stage was rigid, legalistic, and characterized by a sharp cleavage and conflict between "good" and "evil." The ethical intentions of the period were only partially realized, for the repressed "evil" drives broke to the surface in a scapegoat psychology, the cruel treatment of "law-breakers," social upheavals, mass psychic epidemics, and wars.

One of the outcomes of this era, however, was Christianity. It freed Western man from the rigid, legalistic ethic, curtailed the projection of the Self onto kings and leaders by giving every individual an immortal soul, and placed all moral responsibility within that soul. Still, Christianity did not do away with the old moral dualism. It continued to rely on the suppression of "immoral" impulses and refused to take responsibility for the total Self—for the unconscious of the individual and the community.[2] When the Catholic Church regressed to an earlier stage by assuming all moral responsibility for the lives of its communicants and codifying ethics into formulas, the Reformation, in a compensatory reaction, fought to return conscience to the individual.

With the rise of mass man and the authoritarian rule complementary to mass man, the State has taken the place of the Church and now threatens the individual's psychic and moral growth. For undoubtedly it is easier to revert to the primitive security of group consciousness and to project all moral responsibility upon a leader or a State. Aside from its regressive nature, the difficulty with this development is that politicians usually are not chosen on the basis of their moral stature or insight; on the

2. St. Augustine, for example, thanked God that he was not responsible for his dreams.

contrary, they are usually men who are completely unaware of their shadow, living in an illusory orientation of consciousness, and driven by fantasies of power that often end in devastating personal and social catastrophes. The State, on the other hand, is a mere agglomeration of nonentities. If personified, it would be as Hobbes saw it—a monster, consciously, intellectually, and ethically far beneath the level of the individuals composing it, for it represents mass psychology raised to the *nth* degree. This is why Christianity in its best days wanted no part of it and instead set the individual's sights on a kingdom whose foundations are within. The State may be a necessary means for the organization of human life, but when it becomes the primary aim the individual is cheated of his destiny: for then "consciousness, instead of being widened by the withdrawal of projections, is narrowed, because society, a mere condition of human existence, is set up as a goal."[3] Through all the history of mankind, the innate will to consciousness, moral freedom, and culture has proved stronger than the "brute compulsion of projections which keep the individual permanently imprisoned in the dark of unconsciousness and grind him down into nonentity."[4] It appears, therefore, that the conscious achievement of individuality and moral responsibility seems to be man's natural fate. But individuality in itself cannot be the whole aim; otherwise a conglomeration of isolated beings, of mass men, would be the result, and the authoritarian state an inevitable necessity. But this, as we have seen, would really be a retrogression and would not accord with the direction of individual psychic development. For with the rise of individual consciousness and responsibility a new moral advance must follow that will lead to a reunification of the individual and society. This advance would be a product of the understanding that the individual gains of the relationship

3. "Psychotherapy Today," volume 16, p. 107.
4. *Ibid.*, p. 105.

between his consciousness and his unconscious: he would recognize the "evil" within himself and attempt to deal with it; he would no longer repress it and project it onto others or act it out in social convulsions and political movements. Moreover, in the dialogue between his conscious ideals and his unconscious impulses, he would discover and activate a transpersonal entity within his own being that would be able to bridge the gap between his ego personality and humanity as a whole. Once individuals achieve such inner autonomy, there is some hope that the organized accumulation of individuals in a State will no longer be an anonymous mass, but a conscious community. "The indispensable condition for this is conscious freedom of choice and individual decision. Without this freedom and self-determination there is no true community, and, it must be said, without such [a] community even the free and self-secured individual cannot in the long run prosper."[5]

Man's psychic and moral development, therefore, goes hand in hand with his social and political arrangements. Roughly speaking, there are three main patterns of relationship between human beings and government. During the initial period of group psychology there was matriarchy, with its consanguineous community, taboos and customs instead of laws, and no individual differentiation. The rise of male dominance brought patriarchy, with its hierarchical organization, willful rule and repression, and aristocratic distinctions. Today, with the gradual withdrawal of collective projections, there should come, it seems to me, democracy, with voluntary association, consultation and compromise, and equality between individuals, both masculine and feminine.

The development of the nature of morality and of moral decisions follows a similar pattern. In the first period, morality is communal and flows from natural, spontaneous imperatives,

5. *Ibid.,* p. 108.

fears, and expectations. In the second phase it becomes hierarchical, with traditional, legalistically applied precepts supported by external and internal repression. In the third "stage" it is democratic and based on a conscious, nonrepressive acceptance of the total personality. This is why Jung states that the making of an ethical decision today "does not consist in dealing with a given 'material,' but in negotiating with a psychic minority (or majority, as the case may be) that has equal rights. . . . Through the new ethic, the ego-consciousness is ousted from its central position in a psyche organized on the lines of a monarchy or totalitarian state, its place being taken by *wholeness* or the *self.*"[6] And what is true internally is also true externally. For, as Erich Neumann recognized at the end of his study of the history of consciousness, the progressive growth of ego-awareness, the return of collective projections, and the emergence of a personal morality make the leader who is saddled with collective social and moral responsibility an atavism and democracy the form of social organization most suited to the future.[7]

In the end, therefore, here lies one of the essential differences between Jung and Freud. Freud remains mired in a patriarchal and egoistic view of man and morality; consequently, the implications of his psychology are reactionary. From his patriarchal and personalistic view of the unconscious, all he sees is a mass of individuals, each driven by chaotic, aggressive, and egoistic instincts. Hence, for Freud, the preservation and advancement of culture and civilization can only be based on repression both internal, through the firm rule of the superego, and external, through the dictatorship of a leader or the power of the state. Jung, on the other hand, has a conception of the psyche that allows for a natural development of the individual and the society that could lead to a harmonious and democratic resolution of the political and moral conflicts of mankind.

6. Foreword to Neumann, *Depth Psychology and a New Ethic,* pp. 17–18.
7. Erich Neumann, *The Origin and History of Consciousness,* Bollingen Series 42 (Princeton: Princeton University Press, 1954), p. 434.

Index

About the Author

Volodymyr Walter Odajnyk has a Ph.D. in political science from Columbia University, where he taught political theory for five years, and is the author of *Marxism and Existentialism* (1965). He is presently a Diploma Candidate at the C. G. Jung Institute in Zurich.